AF446811

Behind the Mask

Behind the Mask

Kierkegaard's Pseudonymic Treatment
of Lessing in the
Concluding Unscientific Postscript

Michelle Stott

Lewisburg
Bucknell University Press
London and Toronto: Associated University Presses

Associated University Presses
440 Forsgate Drive
Cranbury, NJ 08512

Associated University Presses
25 Sicilian Avenue
London WC1A 2QH England

Associated University Presses
P.O. Box 338, Port Credit
Mississauga, Ontario
L5G 4L8 Canada

The paper used in this publication meets the requirements of the American National Standard for Permanence of Paper for Printed Library Materials Z39.48–1984.

Library of Congress Cataloging-in-Publication Data
Stott, Michelle.
    Behind the Mask : Kierkegaard's pseudonymic treatment of Lessing in the Concluding unscientific postscript / Michelle Stott.
        p.   cm.
    Includes bibliographic references (p. 119–136) and index.
    ISBN 0–8387–5246–2 (alk. paper)
    1. Lessing, Gotthold Ephraim, 1729–1782—Religion. 2. Lessing Gotthold Ephraim, 1729–1782—Philosophy. 3. Kierkegaard, Søren, 1813–1855. Afsluttende uvidenskabelig efterskrift. 4. Kierkegaard, Søren, 1813–1855—Knowledge—Literature. I. Title.
PT2418.R4S76   1993
832'.6—dc20
                                                        92–54945
                                                        CIP

Contents

List of Abbreviations

Kierkegaard's Works

CA	*The Concept of Anxiety*
CI	*The Concept of Irony*
CUP	*The Concluding Unscientific Postscript*
EO	*Either/Or*
FT	*Fear and Trembling*
JP	*Søren Kierkegaard's Journals and Papers*
PF	*The Philosophical Fragments*
PV	*The Point of View for My Work as an Author*
SUD	*Sickness unto Death*
SLW	*Stages on Life's Way*
R	*Repetition*

Lessing's Works

LS	*Lessings Sämtliche Schriften*
HD	*The Hamburg Dramaturgy*
L	*Laokoon*

Acknowledgments

Although many colleagues and friends have contributed input, support and encouragement throughout the writing of this study, I wish to express particular thanks to Dr. Wolff von Schmidt and Dr. Fred Hagen at the University of Utah for their assistance, time, and willingness to discuss my ideas during the early stages of this work. I owe thanks as well to Eva Marie Bates for her invaluable assistance in preparing the extensive translations from German in this text.

Behind the Mask

Introduction

If a poor thinker who is a private practitioner, a cultivator of speculative eccentricities, occupying like a poverty-stricken lodger a garret at the top of a vast building, sat there in his little refuge, held captive in what seemed to him difficult thoughts; . . . if, I say, such a privately practising thinker and speculative crotcheteer were suddenly to make the acquaintance of a man whose renown did not indeed directly insure for him the validity of his thoughts . . . but whose fame was nevertheless like a smile of fortune in the midst of his loneliness, when he found one or two of his difficult thoughts touched upon by the famous man: ah, what joy, what festivity in the little garret chamber.[1]

With these words, Johannes Climacus begins his "Expression of Gratitude," a chapter devoted entirely to a discussion of the German author G. E. Lessing, which is embedded in the *Concluding Unscientific Postscript*. The tone of the text seems to be that of a panegyric which profusely affirms Lessing's individual greatness; at the same time, the ironic undertone negates and retracts all that is said. In the end, the reader is left to wonder why the historical figure of Lessing has been picked up, swathed in ambiguity, and then inserted into the heart of this key philosophical tract.

At least on the surface, it would seem unlikely that enough evidence could be found to convincingly link such apparently dissimilar thinkers as Kierkegaard and Lessing. The mere fact that Lessing is generally acclaimed as the "epitome" of the Enlightenment, whereas Kierkegaard is held to be the "Father of Existentialism," or at least a "preexistentialist" would appear to quite effectively separate the two.

In an external sense, it is possible to find a number of parallels between the lives of Lessing and Kierkegaard: both were reared in a strictly Protestant household and remained closely tied thematically, if not dogmatically, to their Christian upbringing, and both

3

were in frequent conflict with piously authoritarian fathers who could not accept the direction of their son's thought. Both writers lived at a time when the ruling philosophical life-view was fast becoming untenable; both, in fact, helped to strike the final blow that assured the decline of the previous point of view and deflected the current of thought in a new direction. Both thinkers were pioneers whose work and thought defy easy categorization into any specific genre or field. And, in the end, both Lessing and Kierkegaard launched a polemic attack not only against the ossified and stagnating institution of the Lutheran Church, but also against the general lassitude and hypocrisy of a Christianity-grown-rational. These parallels, far from being the result of imitation, conscious or unconscious, on Kierkegaard's part, seem rather to arise as the natural outgrowth of a particular mind-set and personality type shared by the two thinkers. In a sense, Lessing was the vanguard who struggled against the bonds of his century—absolutism, censorship, the necessity of noble patronage for survival as an author—toward the type of independent philosophical and poetic existence that Kierkegaard embodied. In Kierkegaard, one finds the culmination of many forces that Lessing had set into motion almost a century earlier. Nevertheless, these "accidental truths of history" alone are hardly sufficient to explain Lessing's sudden appearance as the key figure in the *Postscript*. Kierkegaard himself provides very little insight in this regard. In fact, outside of the *Postscript* and the *Philosophical Fragments*, Kierkegaard's relationship to and usage of Lessing in the context of his perception of himself and his task as an author seem to be void of any particular significance. In the first entry recorded in the initial volume of his massive journal commentary, Kierkegaard observes that if one is to determinately see a particular light, s/he must first have a supplementary source of illumination, because the position of the first source can only be determined in relationship to the second.[2] The scattered references to Lessing throughout the greater portion of Kierkegaard's journals and published works tend to preserve this purely orientational character. That is, Kierkegaard notes a particular statement or thought by Lessing, addresses it critically, and most often, negatively, then goes on to elaborate his own view of the concept.[3] It is clear that, in this way, some of the ideas propounded by Lessing come to have crucial value in Kierkegaard's own analysis of the relationship of the individual to Christianity. Examples of this would include the notion of the "leap," which finds place in Kierkegaard's thought in a considerably expanded form, and the idea that accidental historical truths can never be proofs for eternal truths of reason. All of these references to Lessing demonstrate an orientational, coolly critical springboard usage of Lessing's thought, which seems quite inconsistent with the general tone of the "Expression of Gratitude" in the *Postscript*.

In spite of this, however, it is a fact that Kierkegaard has asserted in the *Point of View* that the *Postscript* stands as the turning point in his entire work as an author. Given Kierkegaard's powerful subtlety and purpose of construction, it would be unwise to regard Lessing's prominent position in this crucial work as either insignificant or accidental. Strangely enough, very little critical energy has been expended on the actual form in which Lessing appears under Climacus' hand. Most analyses dealing with Kierkegaard's relationship to Lessing focus on a philosophical-theological discussion of actual ideas assimilated by Kierkegaard from Lessing's works; however, little emphasis has been placed on the Lessing figure itself, even though it actually sheds important light on both the nature of the pseudonyms and Kierkegaard's relationship to the pseudonymic figures in his authorship. I would like to submit that the phenomenon of Lessing's appearance in the *Postscript* can only be understood in terms of Kierkegaard's overall concept of existential communication, and his employment of pseudonymous figures in an attempt to fulfill its requirements. In fact, I would assert that the Lessing figure of the *Postscript* is, in actuality, a pseudonymous figure into which Kierkegaard/Climacus has infused that which he believes to be the essential ideality of the historical Lessing. This point of view is radically different from that of critics who maintain that Kierkegaard merely misunderstood or arbitrarily misinterpreted Lessing. The following analysis will, therefore, seek to establish: (1) the actuality of Lessing as a pseudonymic figure in the *Postscript*; (2) the way in which the pseudonymic Lessing figure both corresponds to and differs from the historical Lessing; and (3) the significance of Lessing's pseudonymity in the overall complex of the pseudonyms.

1

Lessing's Actuality as a Pseudonymic Figure

Kierkegaard's Use of Pseudonymic Figures

As a preface to this analysis of Lessing's position as a pseudonymic figure, it would be helpful to briefly review some of the reasons why Kierkegaard felt the pseudonymic form of writing to be a natural, even an essential vehicle for achieving the ends of his authorship.

Throughout the body of his writings, Kierkegaard, in fact, repeatedly endeavors to explain his concept of indirect communication and to justify his employment of the pseudonymous authors and various other figures in his works. Perhaps the most concise exposition of his method of indirect communication, and the purposes that he intends for it to fulfill, is to be found in the *Point of View*.[1] This autobiographical "report to history" was finished during 1848, at which juncture the greater part of the pseudonymous work had already been completed. At the time when he wrote the *Point of View*, Kierkegaard was already turning increasingly to a more direct form of presentation. For this reason, the passionate defense of his earlier works, which is contained in this volume, appears, above all, to be a tacit admission that the tactics he had previously employed had not been successful, since they had been so completely misunderstood that they were now in need of an explanation. As he insists in this volume, however, Kierkegaard felt it necessary to clothe his Christian and philosophical observations in a purely aesthetic or poetical form for two main reasons: (1) the authorship represents his own education to the truth, which, as subjective experience, should never be communicated directly; and, (2) others can be influenced toward a decisively authentic existence only by "deceiving" them indirectly into making a decision, the results and consequences of which will be entirely their own.

In addition to this official explanation for the use of indirect communication, however, any acquaintance with Kierkegaard's journals and papers reveals the fact that the pseudonymic form of writing also gave expression to the author's natural inclination toward and delight in mystification. It is necessary only to leaf through the pages of his journals to find recorded his endless fascination with insanity, deceit, illusion, the secret, the mysterious. The journals also contain numerous references to roles that Kierkegaard himself consciously assumed, roles contrived precisely to deceive any inhabitants of Copenhagen who might be watching the odd habits of this "genius in the market town." In one form or another, these roles that Kierkegaard composed for himself are often reflected in the works of the pseudonymous authors as well.

A further reason for the adoption of indirect communication was the actual dread that Kierkegaard experienced at the thought of direct self-revelation. He often comments on his reluctance to record personal observations in his journal, in fact, going so far as to purposely manipulate the journals with the intent of obscuring and protecting the most inward of his impressions and experiences.[2] Although he craved understanding and interpersonal communication, Kierkegaard frequently suffered a literal blockage to productivity whenever he considered making any direct public statement concerning his works. Indirect communication, therefore, provided an outlet through which he could successfully convey the concepts and perceptions that were of greatest significance to him.

In addition to the points mentioned above, Kierkegaard's boundless respect for Bishop Jacob Peter Mynster seems to have exerted a real censorial influence on his style of presentation. Although Mynster's effect on the authorship should not be overrated, it is a fact that Kierkegaard was hesitant to come into conflict with the Bishop, and postponed for several years his direct polemical attack on the State Church, and Christendom in general, making it public only after Mynster's death. A corollary to this would be Kierkegaard's break with Regine Olsen, and his use of indirect communication out of consideration for her, in his attempt to express to her much that he found himself unable to explain directly.

Whatever the private or public reasons for the adoption of an indirect form of communication may have been, however, and whether or not the pseudonyms actually achieved the desired effect in terms of compelling people to make choices about Christianity, it remains a fact that the pseudonymic style of presentation is particularly well-adapted to the needs of Kierkegaard's authorship. Although the complete mechanics of the pseudonymous works will not be discussed in this study, it can still be observed that there are three main points in which the use of the pseudonymous form proves to be especially useful to Kierkegaard.

(1) Kierkegaard is possessed of a sharply delineated sense of his responsibility as an author to present under his name, only that which finds its existential expression in his own life. As he phrases it:

> I am not permitted to communicate more than I, the speaker, am, that is, in my own factual first person, no more than my life existentially but fairly well conforms to. If I place the requirement higher, I must express that this presentation is a poetic one. (*JP* 6:248 #6528)

And again: "When the demands of ideality are to be presented at their maximum, then one must take extreme care not to be confused with them himself, as if he himself were the ideal" (*JP* 6:181 #6446). For this reason, Kierkegaard adopts the pseudonyms to give himself space to develop a particular life view in all its implications without being required to bear personal responsibility for having an opinion about it. In this sense the pseudonyms serve to "cut loose and provide the elasticity of limitlessness" (*JP* 5:397 #6037). "A pseudonym is excellent for accentuating a point, a stance, a position. He is a poetic person. Therefore it is not as if I personally said: This is what I am fighting for" (*JP* 6:167 #6421). And finally: "I do have one advantage over most authors in that my ideas are always made out in someone's name and are not payable to the bearer; they are made out in someone's name even though I remain anonymous" (*JP* 5:129 #5374).[3] In other words, through the pseudonyms, Kierkegaard is able to endow a series of abstract world-views or attitudes toward life with visible form, and to explore the implications and logical consequences of these views by pushing them to their outermost extremity. But, at the same time, he is relieved of the responsibility of claiming any of these world-views as his own, or of seeming to advocate any of the forms of existence that he depicts. He also gains the freedom to portray levels of ethical and religious commitment far higher than that which he believes himself to have achieved, without danger of seeming to present himself as an example of that particular degree of attainment.

(2) Kierkegaard uses the pseudonymous form to create distance between the author and the reader. Throughout the authorship and the journals, Kierkegaard pours a vast amount of effort into criticism of the preacher, the orator (or author) who:

has rare gifts, and a great understanding of the human passions; [who] knows how to make effective use of the imagination for purposes of delineation; and [who] commands the resources of fear and terror for use in the critical moment of decision. He speaks, and carries the listener with him. The hearer loses himself in engrossed attention, his admiration for the distinguished speaker filling his soul with an almost feminine devotion; he feels his heart beat, his soul is stirred. (*CUP* 16)

This sort of action Kierkegaard brands as sophistry, which "is working in the direction of the animal-category, to work men together into—a crowd" (*JP* 4:219 #4295). Such involvement breeds admiration, a state of being that falls into a purely aesthetic category and demands no personal involvement with the truth. From this sort of oratory arise objective knowledge and dogma that can be learned and repeated by rote, and yet demand no corresponding existential commitment and action.[4]

In contrast to this sort of eloquence that enthralls the listeners or readers until they forget themselves in the sheer artistry which confronts them, Kierkegaard makes every effort to push the readers away, to repel them, to keep them from becoming disciples or mechanically adopting any conclusion. As Walter Kaufmann observes:

His style, however aggravating, is a splendid medium for his purpose. With its epic digressions and its urgency, . . . SK's prose never permits us to lose ourselves in a story or an argument: we are constantly confronted with the author's individuality—and made to think of our own.[5]

In Kaufmann's view, Kierkegaard presents, not a "mirror psychology," but rather a "vortex psychology" that forces us into self-reflection. Instead of confronting us with facts, Kierkegaard makes us aware of our own decisions—he forces questions, not answers, on us. In this way:

he abolishes the untenable analogy of the self with an object or a brute fact that is given and solid, and replaces it with an awareness of possibilities.[6]

In a sense, the retractions, negations and contradictions on the part of the pseudonymous authors and the constant ironic treatment of ideas and situations provoke the same sort of reactions as Bertolt Brecht sought to elicit with his Alienation effect within the medium of Epic Theater. That is, instead of drawing viewers into the dramatic or literary illusion and allowing them to lose themselves in purely emotional identification with the characters and situations of the drama, the author uses every imaginable means to explode the illusion, to remind the viewers at every moment that they are encountering sheer fiction. In this way they are forced to remain emotionally detached from the dramatic action, so a space is created in which, ideally, they can ponder what they see and hear, and decide how they will make changes in their own lives and circumstances. Largely, this distancing or alienation within Kierkegaard's authorship is accomplished through the usage of language itself. As Poul Lübcke points out, indirect communication is not dealing with *semantics*, that is, with the relation of signs to the objects they denote. Rather, it is a question of the *pragmatic* aspect of language—the relation between language users and signs. This kind of pragmatic language concentrates on the task of motivating the listener to choose or act.[7] It is for this reason that Kierkegaard emphasizes the need for double reflection: "The first reflection includes an *understanding* of the meaning of the words, and the second concerns our *interest* in what is being said"—that is, the hearers' decision as to whether they will accept or reject the demands being made upon them.[8]

In this process, the communicator chooses, in Bernard Zelechow's words, "self-consciously difficult modes of discourse in order to force the reader to actively reauthor the authoritative communication." The language of indirect communication destroys "the illusion of a secure relationship to the text which is normally provided by an author as narrator who guides us along the narrow paths of his thinking."[9] Indirect communication, therefore, allows the author as communicator to disappear, while fixing its focus securely on the reader, who is to be in active dialogue with the text. As Robert C. Roberts notes, Kierkegaard "precisely does not want 'to be understood *as Kierkegaard.*' He wants, instead, to be a dispensable vehicle for his reader's coming to understand *other* things."[10] Through the form of presentation, Kierkegaard constantly destroys literary and aesthetic illusion and opens up space between himself and his audience in an attempt to deflect the attention of the readers back onto themselves and their own existence. By this means, he hopes to provoke in them decisions as to how they will respond to the alternatives presented to them through his authorship.[11]

(3) Because the authorship, and particularly the pseudonymous production, leads to no direct conclusions, the whole stands, in Kierkegaard's view, as an effective corrective to the constant systematizing of the Hegelian school and its tendency to present the truth as a body of cut and dried facts.

In addition, Kierkegaard utilizes the pseudonyms to criticize the Hegelian concept of pure being, with its attendant assertion that it is possible through speculative philosophy to directly know the self. From Kierkegaard's standpoint, the attempt to reflect on the self in a speculative mode, in reality removes the individual from the sphere of concrete existence, thus depersonalizing the self into a mere object, a third person caricature or reflected image of true being. According to Kierkegaard, true, direct knowledge of the self can only occur in the presence of an all-knowing God, who alone can make the self transparent to itself. Uncertain as to his own level of self-knowledge, Kierkegaard refuses to present the results of his self-reflection in the first person. In the face of the conviction espoused by advocates of the Hegelian system that they can possess absolute knowledge of the self, Kierkegaard, as a matter of honesty, substitutes the pseudonyms, through which he can explore various aspects of self-knowledge without being forced to claim absolute possession of it.

Kierkegaard's Pseudonyms and Related Figures

Beyond knowing *why* Kierkegaard used pseudonymic figures, in order to understand the Lessing figure, it is necessary to establish *what* these pseudonyms are; that is, what qualities or traits characterize a pseudonymic figure in the authorship. This is a question that, in fact, has received a great deal of critical attention in the decades since the Dane began to publish his works.

In his article "Das Marionettentheater Sören Kierkegaards" (Sören Kierkegaard's Marionette Theater), Martin Thust refers to Kierkegaard as a Master of Reflection who carefully reckons the effect of every word he uses to reveal the passionate inwardness of his thought. Because passion, seen from the outside, is of necessity dramatic, Kierkegaard appears as a dramatist of the religious. In this sense, the dramatist Kierkegaard brings to the stage of his literary works a wealth of figures who, as fragments of life itself, render the various base forms (Urformen) of human existence understandable. Thust then goes on to state that, because the actual theater could not be adapted to his ultimate purposes, Kierkegaard adopted a unique form of marionette theater. Within this theater, Kierkegaard, who himself is a marionette in the hands of the Divine Theater Master, creates puppets who, in turn, form puppets of their own, all of which act and perform in the service of the divine idea.[12] Walter Lowrie, in the introduction to his translation of *Repetition*, decries this concept of a marionette theater as perverse, and states that "one is following a false scent when one seeks to explain S. K.'s use of pseudonyms as a deliberate and artful device."[13] Lowrie's criticism is largely justified, because the concept of marionettes implies a far too mechanical and dependent relationship between the numerous figures that appear in Kierkegaard's works. In addition, a marionette as such contradicts the entire philosophical basis for the authorship. As a subjectively existing thinker, Kierkegaard is most concerned with the inwardness of the individual in opposition to the externality of any objective system. From this standpoint, it is incorrect to postulate marionette figures who are entirely animated and controlled externally, and possess no internal power or personality. Any life or spirit that appears in a marionette is pure illusion, because the puppet is only a painted block of wood until the living hand of the *regisseur* manipulates the strings.

It can be maintained, of course, that Kierkegaard, as the actual author, is that living hand; however, the puppeteer/puppet metaphor is not actually congruent with what Kierkegaard perceives to be his relationship to the figures who inhabit the authorship. He insists repeatedly that he was not involved in a process of "creation" or "construction" as such. Rather, he would like the reader to believe that he, in a sense, put his pen to paper and observed with dispassionate objectivity as the various figures unfolded themselves before his eyes. From this point of view, then, the figures could not be marionettes because they are possessed of their own inner animation and life. Indeed, Kierkegaard constantly relates to them as if they were actually independent creators, and even goes so far as to stipulate that they should at no time be identified with himself and his life.[14] For this reason he insists in "A First and Last Declaration":

> What is written . . . is in fact mine, but only in so far as I put into the mouth of the poetically actual individuality whom I *produced*, his life-view expressed in audible lines. For my relation is even more external than that of a poet, who poetizes characters, and yet in the preface is himself the author. For I am impersonal, or am personal in the second person, a *souffleur* who has poetically produced the *authors*, whose preface in turn is their own production, as are even their own names. So in the pseudonymous works there is not a single word which is mine, I have no opinion about these works except as third person, no knowledge of their meaning except as a reader, not the remotest private relation to them. (*CUP* 551)

At a later point he adds:

> From the beginning I perceived very clearly and do still perceive that
> my personal reality is an embarrassment which the pseudonyms with pa-
> thetic self-assertion might wish to be rid of, the sooner the better, or to
> have reduced to the least possible significance, and yet again with ironic
> courtesy might wish to have in their company as a repellent contrast.
> (*CUP* 552)

If, however, the metaphor of marionettes is to be rejected as too
mechanical and limiting, then the actual essence of the pseudonymous personalities must still be determined. Various critics have
ventured to characterize these figures in a variety of ways. Pierre
Mesnard, for example, employs the term "monad."[15] Stephen Crites
speaks of creatures of fantasy, in which the illusion of individuality
is sustained by the fact that each speaks with a different voice. He
defines the pseudonyms and related figures as theatrical creations,
sheer personae, masks without actors underneath, voices.[16] Georges
Gusdorf speaks of personages in quest of an author, for whom Kierkegaard, a pseudonym himself, is nothing more than the geometric
center of all the figures, the center of gravity for the various viewpoints and thoughts presented.[17] Michael Plekon identifies in the
pseudonyms "case-studies of the self in various activities and stages
of moral and intellectual development."[18] Henning Fenger points
out that through the pseudonyms, Kierkegaard, as "an actor-poet,
who writes his own role, composes the whole army of pseudonyms
with which he has kept other people at a distance from his soul,"
could speak "behind masks and with many tongues. . . . Through all
these roles Kierkegaard (at a safe distance from real life) could give
that brilliant role which was, for him, the role of roles, as the great
genius in the market town of Copenhagen."[19] Josiah Thompson declares in reference to the pseudonymous figures that it is as if Kierkegaard's life had been refracted by a prism into a multitude of
images, each of which retains some mark of the original. To him, the
figures are purely mental, never rooted in the physical world
through bodies; they are disembodied hermits without parents,
home, family, job, appetites, or fears.[20]
Each of these statements describes some facet or view of the immense complexity of pseudonymic existence. In this context, it will
be useful to examine what the pseudonyms say about themselves,
since they present a fairly thorough critique of one another and of
the etherial sphere that they inhabit. It is, of course, a fact that the
standpoints or life-views of the figures are extremely varied, and because each pseudonym is absolutely consistent in his own outlook,
the ideas presented are often in conflict, frequently even dialectical-

ly opposed to one another. And yet, perhaps because the authors are united in the goal of indirectly communicating the truth of inwardness, perhaps, indeed, because of their common state of pseudonymity, there is an openness and sympathy in their assessments of themselves and each other. Although the viewpoints differ, there is a certain similarity or oneness in their perception of their existence as pseudonyms.

For example, a strong tendency toward ironic humility runs through the statements of practically all the pseudonymous authors and editors. One finds Hilarius Bookbinder apologizing for his effrontery in acting like an author.[21] Vigilius Haufniensis admits to his humility of person and lack of pretensions, and even offers to take the name John Brown if his Latin name is of offense to anyone.[22] Johannes de Silentio frankly confesses that he is only an amateur writer with no understanding of philosophy or the Hegelian System.[23] Johannes Climacus declares himself to be one of the lesser folk, for whom it would be far too burdensome to be considered either a hero or an authority (*CUP* 3–6, 546). This type of ironic self-effacement, of course, constitutes an indirect attack on the systematic certainty that characterized the Hegelian School of thought. But behind this assumed abasement, there is a real strain of honest self-appraisal and a realistic absence of illusion in relation to the self. That is, the pseudonyms never pretend to be anything other than that which they are. Their overpowering dialectical consciousness will not allow them to believe that they are anything other than pseudonyms. They are always acutely aware of their limitations, and of their distance from actuality. Thus, we find that Frater Taciturnus admits his inability to bestow flesh and blood on the character of his creation (*SLW* 365). Likewise, Constantine Constantius reflects that at the utmost he can imagine a poet, but he cannot become one, because that lies beyond the boundaries of his essential standpoint (*R* 154). In the same sense, he also records his incapacity to follow the young man in making a religious movement (*R* 94–95). The Quidam of "Guilty?/Not Guilty?" ends the diary of his most intense passion with the words "It deals with nothing" (*SLW* 362), while William Afham ironically asserts, "But who then am I? Let nobody ask. . . .I am not worth asking about, for I am the most insignificant of all things. . . .I am 'pure being' and therefore almost less than nothing" (*SLW* 93). Johannes Climacus, in his critique of all the pseudonymous works previous to the *Postscript* constantly refers to the other authors singly and as a group as pseudonyms—that is, he in no way attempts to convince the reader that these might in actuality be historically existing authors, a ruse one might expect if the pseudonyms were being employed in the traditional sense of a *nom de plume*. In this review, Climacus speaks at times of the other authors as if they were existing individuals ("Had the author of the *Stages* consulted me" [*CUP* 253]; "whether this has been clear to the author . . . I cannot tell" [*CUP* 230], etc.). And yet at another point he refers to them almost as tools when he remarks that, in addition to what they are directly, the pseudonyms indirectly constitute a polemic against speculative philosophy (*CUP* 243). Climacus does not hesitate to define the other pseudonyms according to the standpoint that they embody (Constantine is case-hardened understanding, Victor is sympathetic irony, the Seducer is perdition in cold blood, etc.), and remarks that they are each consistent to the point of despair (*CUP* 264). He also states quite openly of Johannes de Silentio that:

> it would have been impossible to represent this existential collision in an existing individuality. . . . Johannes *de silentio* is therefore not himself such an existing individual; he is a reflective consciousness who . . . repeatedly runs himself into a collision with the understanding, while the lyricism of the book results from the reaction. (*CUP* 234)

After, however, in this way objectively referring to Johannes de Silentio as a reflective consciousness rather than an existing individuality, Climacus concludes as if the other pseudonym were, indeed, such an existing being by stating, "How things really are with Johannes *de silentio* I cannot of course tell with certainty, since I do not know him personally." (*CUP* 234)

The question of whether or not the actual conclusions that the various figures draw concerning particular philosophical standpoints are correct moves beyond the focus of this inquiry. The important point here is that the figures understand and accept themselves as pseudonyms, as reflective consciousness that is not and cannot be existing individuality, as the embodiment of specific viewpoints who cannot go beyond the limits of their own particular stance. Within the boundaries of their existence, however, they quite openly compare themselves with other pseudonyms, analyzing and criticizing their own standpoints as well as those of the others.[24]

In particular the two thought experiments (*Repetition* and "Guilty?/Not Guilty?" in *Stages*) provide extremely valuable insight into the essence of the pseudonyms and their related figures. In a very significant sense, the relationship between creator and creation in these experiments illuminates Kierkegaard's own perceived connection with the figures that populate his works. To begin with, it must be pointed out that there is not a single instance in which the creator refers to his creation as a lifeless object, a puppet to be manipulated at will, a mechanism controlled by the creator. Quite to the contrary, the creators consistently relate to the figures that they experiment as if these were living personalities. In the course of his story, for example, Constantine speaks of the way he drew the young man to himself, taught him to confide, and enticed his melancholy from him (*R* 7). Although Constantine exhorts the young man to a particular course of action (*R* 22–23), the young man chooses not to carry it through, and even disappears for a period of time, which causes Constantine quite a deal of concern (*R* 27, 84). At various points, Constantine exclaims that the young man does injustice if he thinks he has been forgotten (by Constantine) (*R* 84), and that he (Constantine) is not indifferent to his young friend, as the young man fears (*R* 154). Thus, even in his lengthy analysis of the experiment, Constantine continues to refer to the young man as a self-existing individuality.

Although the Frater is not personally involved in his protagonist's story, and therefore the relationship does not stand out in such sharp relief, still he relates to the Quidam as to a self-activated individual, in the same manner as Constantine to his young man. In fact, in empathizing with imagined readers who might complain at the length of Quidam's diary, the Frater agrees that it is written with great prolixity: "how copiously indeed . . . no one knows better than I, who often exhausted, often bored, have been tempted to let him alone and lose patience" (*SLW* 363). The Frater also states that he is not writing in order to convince the Quidam, but rather to remark on something true in him, to let him pass for what he is (*SLW* 367). On one occasion, he does refer to the Quidam as a "manikin," but that is only as a possible negative objection raised by hypothetical readers (*SLW* 363).

Nevertheless, it is clear in both cases that the two young men, and the women with whom they relate, are creatures of imagination, experimental characters. In fact, the Frater specifically discusses the fact that his protagonist does not exist outside the experiment, which is, in his opinion, fortunate, because the young man's attitudes would only be ridiculed in real existence (*SLW* 367).

In the statements of the creators concerning their creations, there is a marked absence of words commonly connected with construction (i.e., to make, to plan out, to invent, etc.). For example, as Constantine states, "The young man whom I have *brought into being* is a poet" (*R* 154. Emphasis added). And later, "At the first glance, I *saw* that he was a poet" (*R* 159. Emphasis added). The Frater refers to "the figure which here is *conjured up*" (*SLW* 363. Emphasis added). Constantine's further remarks become even more revealing.

He records that in this experiment he is only a *serviceable spirit*, and that his apparent indifference to the young man was only a misunderstanding to which he gave occasion in order by this means to *bring him out* (*R* 154. Emphasis added). He further states:

> Every movement I have made is made only in order to *throw light upon him*; I have constantly had him *in mente,* every word of mine is either ventriloquism or is uttered with reference to him . . . what I say about myself one is to understand obscurely of him. . . .Thus I have done for him what I could. (*R* 154–55. Emphasis added)

And further:

> the young man is the focus of interest, whereas I am a transitory figure, like a midwife in relation to the child she has brought to birth. And such in fact is my position, for I have as it were *brought him to birth*, and therefore as the older person I do the talking. *My personality is a presupposition psychologically necessary to force him out.* . . . I have often had to *tease him in order that he might make himself visible.* (*R* 158–59. Emphasis added)

Frater Taciturnus also speaks of arranging his work so that the Quidam could be adequately *illuminated* and *taught* to exert himself (*SLW* 363. Emphasis added).

From the above passages, it becomes clear that the creator must, in a sense, draw the personality out of the dialectical tension of thought and, once having set it in motion, allow it to roll on, propelled by the force of its own consistency. From this point, it is necessary, further, to arrange circumstances and surroundings so that the figure he has thus coaxed out will be able to show up most clearly. Not to create individuality, but to bring individuality forth out of the realm of thought and to allow it "to exist in all [its] possibility" (*SLW* 395) is the task of the creator, the experimenter, the pseudonymous authorship.[25]

At this point it is necessary to attempt an identification of the substance of these conjured figures. Once again, a great deal of enlightenment can be gained from the figures themselves, in their sleepless self-consciousness. The first clue is furnished by the young aesthete in *Either/Or* when he observes:

> Back of the world in which we live, far in the background, lies another world. The relation between the two is not unlike the relation we sometimes see in the theater between the forestage scene in the regular acting

area and a scrim scene projected behind it. Through a thin gauze we
see, as it were, a world of gauze, lighter, more ethereal, qualitatively
different from the actual world. (*EO* 1:302)

In reality, this world of gauze hidden behind the actual world like
a "face behind a face" (*EO* 1:173) is the sphere inhabited by the
pseudonymous figures. That their existence is "lighter," "more ethereal" and "qualitatively different" becomes clear in the statements of
the authors concerning themselves. For example, William Afham
states:

I am the pure being which is the accompaniment of everything yet never
observable, because I am constantly *aufgehoben*. I am like the line
above which is written the task for the pupil to reckon out, and below it
the answer—who cares about the line? I myself am not capable of doing
anything whatever. (*SLW* 93)[26]

Through its use of Hegelian vocabulary, this statement constitutes a
direct attack on Hegel's concept of pure being. However, the implications extend far beyond the anti-Hegelian polemic. For all
William's apparent humility, it must be pointed out that this insignificant line *is that* which illuminates the problem as an actual problem,
where, otherwise, it might not be recognized as such. And so it is
with all the pseudonymous figures, who in the airy nothingness of
pure being delineate the problem as a problem.

And yet there is another, more significant aspect to the essence of
the pseudonyms. In the *Philosophical Fragments*, Johannes Climacus says of himself, "I have disciplined myself and keep myself
under discipline, in order that I may be able to execute a sort of nimble dancing in the service of Thought, so far as possible also to the
honor of the God, and for my own satisfaction." He then continues:

I have only my life, and the instant a difficulty offers I put it in play.
Then the dance goes merrily, for my partner is the thought of Death, and
is indeed a nimble dancer; every human being, on the other hand, is too
heavy for me. Therefore I pray, *per deos obsecro*: Let no one invite
me, for I will not dance.[27]

This statement is further illuminated by a companion passage from
Kierkegaard's own "First and Last Declaration" in the *Postscript*.
There he condemns anyone who is "unacquainted with the educative
effect of companionship with an ideality which imposes distance"
and further decries anyone who has "*really* made a fool of himself by

having to drag the weight of my personal reality instead of having the doubly reflected, light ideality of a poetically actual author to dance with" (*CUP* 553).

The pseudonymous figures, then, consist of pure ideality, which has been released from all human heaviness (systems, dogma, opinions, historical facts and events, admiring disciples, etc.) and, thus, is light enough to dance nimbly through the realm of thought. And yet it is this very lightness that makes it possible to render the actual challenges and conflicts of inwardness visible.[28] In this context, Paul Holmer seems to capture the pseudonymic sphere of being quite succinctly when he asserts that Kierkegaard's literature presents:

> idealized persons . . . who are more distinct than historical personages; and their oppositions, polemical postures, and criteria are thereby brought into sharper focus and a tighter compass. His literature both compresses human circumstances and distills the consequences of the forms of life we all choose, so that we can get a more acute picture of what is involved.[29]

With the foregoing established, it will now be possible to investigate Kierkegaard's relationship to Lessing.

Lessing as a Pseudonymic Figure

It is the thesis of this analysis that Lessing, as he appears in the *Postscript*, is in actuality a pseudonymous figure, and, therefore, a figure of pure ideality as discussed above. In reality, there is no figure in the entire authorship that has its being in any other category than pure ideality. This includes Socrates, Abraham, Job, and even Kierkegaard himself in the signed works, since, as Kierkegaard explicitly states, he, too, is a pseudonym molded by the divine hand of Governance.[30] However, although several critical analyses of the connection between Kierkegaard and Lessing have been written, none recognizes the pseudonymous reality of the Lessing figure as it is presented by Climacus.

As might perhaps be expected, many of the more prominent discussions of the Lessing/Kierkegaard relationship have centered entirely on an analysis of the theological and philosophical points raised by Kierkegaard through his depiction of Lessing. The inquiries by Richard Campbell,[31] Jacques Colette,[32] Gordon Michalson,[33] and James Whisenant[34] fall into this category. Although each affords insight into the questions raised by the "Theses Possibly or Actually Attributable to Lessing" and related ideas, the writers do not comment specifically on the figure of Lessing itself.

Of the critics who do approach the historical Lessing, Paul Requadt[35] essentially provides a description, first of Lessing, and then of the pictures of Lessing presented by Schlegel and Kierkegaard, but he draws no wide-ranging conclusions concerning the way in which Lessing is portrayed by either of the other two authors.

Both Claus von Bormann[36] and Hans-Martin Gerlach[37] begin their articles by isolating certain similarities of life experience, which may have drawn Kierkegaard's interest to Lessing: von Bormann points out the isolation, independence, and lack of close friends common to both authors, while Gerlach shows that each employed an ironic form of writing to combat dogma and the rigidity of church structure, and each struggled against a closed philosophical system (Lessing against Christian Wolff and his followers, Kierkegaard against the Hegelian school). From this basic framework, however, Gerlach and von Bormann leave the historical Lessing and turn to an investigation of the theoretical similarities and differences between the two authors: von Bormann enters into the question of history through an analysis of Lessing's and Kierkegaard's respective views on tragedy, whereas Gerlach contrasts Lessing's conception of truth with that propounded by Kierkegaard.

Erik Lunding[38] offers, perhaps, the most complete investigation of the correspondences between the historical Lessing and Kierkegaard's portrayal of the German author. In his analysis, Lunding observes that Kierkegaard seems to find in Lessing a sort of spiritual brother, and then asks whether Kierkegaard's view of Lessing involves only self-identification, or whether it is possible to isolate any sort of objective interpretation underlying the Lessing figure. Lunding then goes on to present various examples of Kierkegaard's apparently willfully subjective usage of Lessing. Chief among these examples is Kierkegaard's response to a particular letter written by Lessing to Moses Mendelssohn. As Lunding observes:

> In this case, however, it is not even a concern for Kierkegaard to "understand" Lessing's reasoning. . . . In this manner he succeeds through his passionate, egocentric thinking, in relating everything to his own tale of suffering.[39]

Lunding also points out essential differences between Lessing's usage of "the leap" and Kierkegaard's employment of the same term, and concludes, "None of this is mentioned by Kierkegaard, so that

the uniformity of his image of Lessing will not be disturbed."[40] At
various points in his discussion, Lunding chides Kierkegaard for his
failure to openly debate certain points with Lessing, and for the fact
that most often Lessing's ideas are transformed in some manner
when they enter the Kierkegaardian sphere. As he notes, Kierkegaard's view of Lessing seems to reflect Lessing's inner life and
struggles rather than his actual life and writings. He then continues:

> Since therefore the image of Lessing provided in the "Postscript" corre-
> sponds to this ideal, the question of the purely scientific truth- and reality-
> content of such a Lessing interpretation obtrudes itself immediately onto
> the reader. It has already been proven that Kierkegaard in his great Les-
> sing portrayal is not able to manage without suppressions and distor-
> tions.[41]

In Lunding's opinion, these failings should not eclipse the value of
the psychological insight attained by Kierkegaard's particular interpretation. However, as Lunding states further:

> Kierkegaard's insights into Lessing's work are obviously not the expres-
> sion of a cool, objective-scientific attitude; to the contrary, such a radi-
> cal assimilation of the other person's stock of ideas has taken place, that
> it has become an integral part of his own world.[42]

Lunding concludes his article with the observation that Lessing
moved in circles which were in constant contact with the budding
ideas of German Idealism. In contrast, Kierkegaard fought inces-
santly to rid his age of the encumbering inherited baggage of that
same system. Therefore:

> Only in the forms of thought can extensive correspondences and similar-
> ities be ascertained. These similarities are rooted in universal human
> possibilities, namely in the mutual endeavor to strip oneself of an imper-
> sonal mass existence, in order to realize naked existence at the brink of
> isolation, in subjective truth.[43]

Although Lunding does, indeed, contribute important insight into
the Lessing/Kierkegaard question, his article seems, nevertheless, to
be plagued with a basic confusion that leads him, at times, into criticism of Kierkegaard's procedure, which does not really apply to the
question at hand. That is: (1) Even beneath Lunding's praise of
Kierkegaard, one can detect a certain affronted criticism of the Dan-

ish writer's flagrant omission of any "objective," scientific, factual presentation of Lessing. (2) Lunding constantly confuses Kierkegaard's treatment of Lessing the man with his assimilation of Lessing's ideas, as if the two were identical or interchangeable. (3) Lunding remains shackled to the figure of the historical Lessing throughout his entire exposition.

(1) It very quickly becomes clear in a study of Kierkegaard's practice as an author and thinker, that he is singularly uninterested in academic or scientific research regarding the figures presented in the authorship. In fact, he constantly levels criticism at the "assistant professors" and systematizers who are involved in just such objective, scientific investigation. At no point in either the published works or the collected papers does Kierkegaard demonstrate the slightest concern for a factual, scientific background to any person or figure with whom he is concerned. Even the extensive consideration of Socrates in *Concept of Irony* presents an inner ideality rather than an external historicity. Therefore, it is useless to criticize Kierkegaard for his lack of cool, scientific objectivity when, by choice and inherent creativity, that method of procedure was closed out from the very beginning. That is, it was never his intention to be scientific in his presentation.[44]

(2) From the foregoing discussion of the pseudonyms, it has become clear that the method of the thought experiment, and, on a larger scale, the entire pseudonymous authorship, was to coax a character out of the dialectic and then allow it to develop under the force of its own inwardness. Because of Kierkegaard's heavy emphasis on the category of the subjectively existing individual, that which one *is* takes on supreme importance. This same emphasis on *being* is reflected in the pseudonymous figures. The consistency and integrity of each figure stands in and of itself. By combining an exposition of the characteristics of the Lessing figure with a discussion of philosophical doctrine, Lunding is essentially trying to mix eggs and oranges—he is treating two very different categories as if they were the same. In reality, the pseudonymous figure of Lessing has an entirely different function in the *Postscript* than do the theses attributable to Lessing. That is, the theses provide *content* for the philosophico-religious discussion that occupies the greater portion of the book, whereas the Lessing figure serves as a *visual concretion* of the concept of the subjectively existing individual.[45] The Lessing of the *Postscript* is the line that illuminates the problem as an actual problem, whereas the theses apply to the problem itself.

(3) It is the historical actuality of G. E. Lessing which contributes the human ballast which, according to Climacus, is too heavy to

allow him to perform his nimble dancing in its presence. In this sense, Lunding and other critics who maintain a purely historical point of view in relationship to Kierkegaard's Lessing put themselves in the position of "having to drag the weight" of Lessing's "personal reality" instead of having the "doubly reflected, light ideality" of the poetically actual Lessing to dance with (*CUP* 553). If this ideality is accepted, the critical confusion and conflict promptly disappear.

What remains to be shown, then, is that this light, pseudonymic ideality does, in fact, exist as the essence of Kierkegaard's Lessing figure. In this respect, we are fortunate, because Climacus does not simply present the finished figure to us. Instead, he proceeds step-by-step to strip away the historical heaviness, thus allowing the ideality to emerge into concrete visualization before the reader.

The "Expression of Gratitude" in the *Postscript* begins with Climacus in his garret, laden with difficult thoughts, shuddering before his suspicion that there is a weakness in the foundation of the vast building on which he is perched. Suddenly, in the midst of his loneliness and philosophic isolation, Climacus makes acquaintance with a man of renown, who in his own thought has touched on some of the difficult ideas with which Climacus himself labors. Following an ironic introduction, Climacus initiates the process of separating the historical from the ideal essence with the open, straightforward observation that "this expression of gratitude does not relate to what is ordinarily, and I assume also rightly, admired in Lessing" (*CUP* 60). At the outset, therefore, Climacus makes it clear that the traits that will appear in his Lessing will be other than what one would expect in a traditional view of the German thinker. Climacus then proceeds with his separative surgery:[46]

- My admiration does not have to do with Lessing as a scholar,

- nor relate to what appeals to me as a brilliant myth: that he was a librarian;

- it does not have to do with what seems well-nigh an epigram: that he was the soul in a library,

- that he held possession of an enormous learning in an almost omnipresent autopsy, a gigantic apparatus kept under the control of thought and obedient to every hint of the spirit, pledged to the service of the Idea.

- It does not have to do with Lessing as a poet,

- nor relate to his mastery in the construction of the dramatic sentence,

- his psychological power in poetic revelation of the secrets of the mind,

- his hitherto unexcelled gift of dramatic dialogue, which in his hands moves freely and unembarrassed in an easy conversational tone, though heavily freighted with thought.

- It does not have to do with Lessing as an aesthetician,

- nor relate to that line of demarcation which at his command (quite otherwise authoritative than a papal bull) was drawn between poetry and the formative arts;

- nor does it relate to that wealth of aesthetic observation which was his, and which continues to suffice even in our own age.

- Nor, again, does it have to do with Lessing as sage;

- nor does it relate to that genial wisdom which was his, and which modestly concealed itself in the unpretentious dress of the fable.

In this manner, within the space of a single page, Climacus has divorced from Lessing everything that is usually cited as the mark of his greatness: his work as a scholar and librarian, his poetic and dramatic artistry, his psychological insight and perception, his aesthetic observation. One would be tempted to remark that nothing remains which actually was Lessing. And, in the sense of historical factuality, this is true. The externally recognizable form of Lessing has been removed. But Kierkegaard, working through Climacus, is interested neither in externals, nor in the weight of historicity. That which fascinates him is the hidden, inexpressible inwardness, which he senses emanating from beneath the factuality of Lessing's life and works. That which he seeks lies underneath the actions, between the written words and pages, behind Lessing's own ambivalent and often confusing mask. As Climacus continues his analysis, "my admiration has to do with something else, something such that its very nature makes it impossible to admire it directly, or establish through one's admiration any immediate relationship with Lessing; for his merit consists precisely in his having prevented it" (*CUP* 60 – 61). Having methodically sliced away the heaviness of human historicity, Climacus now proceeds to postulate the essence of pure ideality that he has distilled from the historical Lessing. From Climacus' ideal characterization, it is possible to isolate three predominant traits that form the basis for the Lessing figure. (1) Lessing is a subjectively existing thinker who, almost like Socrates, insures himself against fellowship and prevents discipleship. (2) He, through his silence and calculated withdrawal into himself, offers no results, develops no system, presents nothing which thoughtless adherents could repeat by rote. (3) He communicates in an ironic form calculated to confuse and dismay the unwary.

Section II pursues each of these themes, in turn, with reference to the individual assertions made by Climacus in the "Expression of Gratitude."

2

How the Pseudonymic and Historical Lessing Figures Correspond and Differ

Even a cursory reading of Kierkegaard very quickly reveals the fact that the concept of subjectivity, with its corollary emphasis on the individual, stands at the very heart of Kierkegaardian thought. For this reason, it is significant that Lessing is the figure employed to introduce the most comprehensive philosophical development and discussion of subjectivity in the entire authorship. With the exception of Socrates, Lessing is, in fact, the only major secular historical individual who is accorded a place in the Kierkegaardian gallery of characters. This section will, therefore, analyze the pseudonymic Lessing figure in relationship to the historical Lessing. This investigation will be carried out in reference to the guiding hypothesis of this study, which is that Climacus makes visible in the Lessing figure that which he perceives to be the essence of true ideality, which he has distilled from the substance of the historical Lessing. Only the data are presented in this section; an analysis of the information follows in the third section.

Section I: Lessing as a Subjectively Existing Thinker

Lessing is a subjectively existing thinker who, almost like Socrates, insures himself against fellowship and prevents discipleship.

In order to adequately discuss this assertion, this statement is divided into three sections: (a) the notion of subjectivity, (b) the God-relationship, and (c) the concept of discipleship.

Subjectivity

Reference has previously been made to Kierkegaard's conception of himself as a corrective for his age. His own conviction was that one voice could do very little to actually change the course of social development. And yet he felt it to be his duty to proclaim to contemporary civilization the fact that it was about to founder, and to forcefully challenge society to reevaluate itself and its mode of existence.[1] In Kierkegaard's view, the modern age was one of dissolution,[2] a period in which humanity had become:

> hyper-reflective, abstract, given to mindless chatter and endless deliberation. It was a time of lethargy and self-satisfaction. . . .Moderns were superficially knowledgeable, ethically ambiguous and hungry for innovation, thus easily manipulated by journalistic sensationalism and programs for reform.[3]

One of the most critical dangers inherent in the time was, according to Kierkegaard, that which he perceived as "Hegelianism's apotheosis of the state and civil society"[4]; that is, the tendency toward self-deification exhibited by society and its institutions. As he states: "The crowd is sick for power and considers itself fortified against all reprisals, for how is it possible to get hold of the crowd" (*JP* 4:141 #4118). And even more strongly: "The idol, the tyrant, of our age is 'the many,' 'the crowd,' statistics" (*JP* 3:317 #2951). In Kierkegaard's view, this "massification of society is the flip side of its secularization"[5]; the vacuum left by increasing secularization does not long remain empty, since the self-deifying crowd becomes the new idol, a diabolical and "demonic" religion.[6] In this sense, Kierkegaard "seeks to un-socialize the individual in order to un-deify society."[7]

As Kierkegaard views it, mass society or the "herd" is "the offspring of a passionless age, committed only to self-interest."[8] This "herd" betrays:

> the increasingly total absence of ideals from social life, though a lot of talk about God remains. . . .The herd is Kierkegaard's name for the disease that occurs when people only incompletely adhere to Christianity, retaining its metaphysics while repudiating its morality.[9]

Society thus falls into decay as it loses contact with the idea, with Christian ideals; it becomes "spiritless," lacking in intellectual, ethical and religious individualism.[10] The "crowd" or "herd" fosters those who confuse "socialization with salvation" and who believe their existential task to be completed when they have undergone the initiation rites prescribed by society, such as marriage, the completion of one's education, and the entrance into a career.[11] In Kierkegaard's opinion, "a crowd in its very concept is the untruth, by reason of the fact that it renders the individual completely impenitent and irresponsible." (*PV* 112); he has only condemnation for the "individual who flees for refuge into the crowd, and so flees in cowardice from being an individual." (*PV* 113). A crowd, as a collective abstraction, can always elude the moral imperative of Christianity, which demands that a person act in accordance with what he or she believes; the crowd suppresses the individual, who alone is capable of accepting responsibility under God, and who can make valid judgements.[12] In this sense, the concept of the "faceless mass" is the very antithesis of the strenuous demand of Christianity that one stand face to face with oneself before God. Kierkegaard's answer to those who crave the sort of concealment mentioned above is entirely unequivocal:

> How hypocritical! No, it is cowardice, and moreover it is whimpering and whining in order always to manage to be many—and one never dares to be alone, never dares to be an *I*. But if it is a "cause," then there are many right away—and there is protection first of all against the danger we fear most in our wretched, wretched, demoralized age—to be alone, to be a solitary *I*. (*JP* 3:486 #3219)

The existing individual stands unquestionably as the most basic building block of Kierkegaardian thought, that which he repeatedly denotes as the decisive Christian category.[13] "Existence," however, in this sense, can never be equated with the passive sense of merely being alive and breathing. As Stephen Evans explains, existence in Kierkegaard's thought is equivalent to choosing and acting. It is, therefore, a process of actualizing or "duplicating" particular ethical-religious possibilities in one's life. Kierkegaard is not interested in an epistemological investigation of the nature of truth in general. Rather, his question concerns a particular type of truth, which is essentially related to existence. Thus, the prime question of his thought becomes "How do I exist true-ly" or, in other words, "How do I achieve a mode of existence that is truth?" Evans continues:

> What Kierkegaard says about this question is that a person does not

exist truly merely by *knowing* what is objectively true. It is possible for
a person to objectively apprehend the truth without allowing the truth to
transform his existence.[14]

This idea that truth must effect an active alteration or change in
one's existence seems to best capture the Kierkegaardian sense of
subjectivity. Truth is not merely something to be known, to be reflected upon and speculated about. It is something to be actualized.
As various critics have pointed out, if an individual is to exist in
truth, everything external must be transformed into something internal. Subjective existence is thus far more profoundly concerned
with the *how* than with the *what* of truth.[15]
In Kierkegaard's view, the Creator has endowed every person with
a certain individuality and distinctiveness, and the real meaning of
life lies in fulfilling this uniqueness. In fact, Kierkegaard declares
that one's entire salvation lies in becoming an individual, an independent *I* (*JP* 3:489 #3225). For this reason he strongly decries the
tendency of men and women in his age to drift along as impersonal
faces in the crowd, anonymous entities who will not risk the effort to
become actively and decisively involved in existence. As he complains: "Anonymity has . . . demoralized the time in this way, that
by doing away with persons with character it has contributed to ren-
dering the age characterless" (*JP* 3:728 #3728). And further: "The
fact is that no one in our day dares to be a person. . . .From fear of
the others, one dares not be an *I* and therefore strives to become an
impersonal something, a cause, the cause, a principle, and the like"
(*JP* 3:486 #3219).
Particularly in light of later popular interpretations of "Existentialism," individuality and subjectivity, it is important to stress the
fact that Kierkegaard at no point understands these key concepts in
terms of "the accidental, the angular, the selfish, the eccentric, and
so forth" (*CUP* 117). Kierkegaard's individualism, as David Fletcher shows, has often been described as "asocial," as "intensely individualistic in a romantic sense, glorying in the primacy of the
individual's interior life and guided by a self-directed ethic that
finds no basis for its decisions outside of the individual.[16] However,
although in the usual interpretation of the concept, an intense subjectivity would seem to imply a personal withdrawal from society at
large, in reality, individuals who attempt to develop this true Christian
inwardness and passionate subjectivity in no sense retreat into a
solipsism that cuts them off from the world. Quite to the contrary,
the subjective individual "finds himself *immersed* in the world and in
relation to others." In this sense, for example, the "stages" that are

so basic to Kierkegaardian thought present far more than mere "alternative inner attitudes"; rather, they illustrate "ways of living in the world and relating to others."[17] Kierkegaardian thought provides no license to indulge the self without consideration for others, or for society in general. The individual is construed as a principle of action, whose challenge is to achieve the *proper sort* of subjectivity, which consists in "intensified 'inwardness', passionate personal commitment, and personal decision and responsibility for what one is and does."[18]

That the individual is, in fact, at all times deeply related to the community becomes clear in Kierkegaard's assertion that:

> the single individual is dialectically decisive as the presupposition for forming *community*, and in *community* the single individual is qualitatively something essential. . . .The cohesiveness of community comes from each one's being a single individual, and then the idea; the connectedness of a public or rather its disconnectedness consists of the numerical character of everything. Every single individual in community guarantees the community; the public is a chimera. (*JP* 3:318 #2952)

In this sense, as Merold Westphal points out, the individual and society stand in a relation of dialectical interaction with one another, each mutually determined by the other. Thus, the individual reflects the society and vice versa—"the primacy of passion or reflection in the individuals who make up society will be an index of that society's shape."[19] Fletcher notes further that individuals must relate first to God, and then they will be able to unite with others to form a community. True membership in a community is only possible when the individual has first gained his or her own ethical bearing.[20]

The foundational point of reference in Kierkegaard's thought is Christianity. As a corrective to the "spiritlessness," the leveling and degradation of the individual prevalent in society, he believes that individuals must take action and relate themselves to an unconditioned source of values—that is, to God. Because this source lies outside of humanity, it provides a permanent reference point and a true source of stability for the individual.[21] This God-relationship automatically excludes the type of subjectivity that appears as an irrational and selfish expression of personal desires and opinions. Within the bounds of Christianity, subjectivity is the intense focus on existence that leads the subject to apply every moral and religious injunction to him- or herself. The result of this appropriation is that such subjects are constantly involved in the process of self-examination to determine whether or not their actions measure up to divine expectations.[22] Fletcher indicates in this context that Kierkegaard's standing is not unsocial, because it is "precisely as an individual that man's social responsibility truly becomes a possibility."[23] Such an individual will not speak of justice while refusing to carry it out, as happens in the "crowd." Rather, "the individual will risk his personal stake in life to make a contribution to social life."[24] Therefore, in terms of social concerns, what is needed is not political action, but rather the results that the solitary individual can bring about through developing the religious dimension of life.[25] For this reason, Kierkegaard consistently advocates the internal reform of the individual, rather than external political action. In his words, "every future effort at reformation, if the person involved is a true reformer, will be directed against 'the crowd,' not against the government" (*JP* 4:140 #4116). The truth, or idea, which the crowd cannot attain as a collective, is available to every individual. Thus, only the God-relationship can truly make all humans equal, and religion alone is entitled to the claim to "true humanity."[26]

In the Kierkegaardian sense, then, an authentic subjective existence is one in which belief and action are congruent. This requirement forms the basis for Kierkegaard's assertion that there were no Christians in Christendom: that is, although people were baptized, and could repeat their catechism of faith by rote, there was very little actualization of these beliefs in daily life and action. Kierkegaard was particularly critical of the clergy on this point. In his opinion, preachers could always be found gesticulating gracefully with their hands while they delivered eloquent—but empty—sermons. He demanded instead that individuals gesticulate with their lives, that they reduplicate in action the truths expounded in the sermons.[27] It is because of the demand for actualization of Christian values and truths in one's existence that Kierkegaardian subjectivity serves to heighten responsibility to the utmost, so that every action is endowed with immense eternal significance. In Kierkegaard's words:

From the purely human point of view the most prudent thing is always to make life as trivial as possible (as devoid of ideas, as spiritless or as devoid of spirit as possible)—for the more mediocre, the easier life becomes.

Yet one deceives himself if he thinks this way. For this very reason Christianity approaches from the opposite side and makes man responsible—to the accounting of eternity—for whether or not he has applied the Christian criterion to his life. (*JP* 4:247 #4348)

As has been mentioned, in Kierkegaardian terms, subjectivity, with its attendant passionate involvement in existence, culminates in the individual relationship with God, who is the ultimate and absolute subjectivity. Kierkegaard believes that direct communication of inner experience—and particularly, inner God-experience—is impossible: individuals cannot express their subjective inwardness to others through the medium of words. One can relate directly only to God, who focuses on individuals, and, as pure subjective spirit, can communicate directly with the spirit of the inward-turning person. Since God is himself the Truth, there can be no communication of truth without his help and involvement. That is, "God is at once the Truth and the middle term which renders it intelligible" (*PV* 117–18). At various points throughout the authorship, Kierkegaard refers to this truth relationship through the medium of God as a type of inner deepening, as spiritual transparency, and as intense illumination.[28]

It is in relationship to truth that the conflict between Kierkegaardian subjectivity and the prevalent objectivity of the age becomes most apparent. Objectivity by definition is impartial and neutral, presupposing a personal noninvolvement with the matter or object under consideration.[29] In contrast, however, "Subjectivity is inwardness. Inwardness is spirit. To believe is not an *indifferent relation to something* which is true, but an *infinitely decisive relation to something*" (*JP* 4:346 #4537). In other words, truth, "as relation of unity with the ultimate reality, i.e., God," can be attained only by becoming radically subjective. The reason for this is quite clear:

> The ultimate reality is God; and a person can place himself in a relation to this ultimate reality only by suspending his reason and making a "leap of faith." Making a "leap of faith" requires, not objectivity and rationality, but "passion." And passion is something essentially non-rational and subjective.[30]

It would, of course, be a gross misunderstanding to claim that Kierkegaard's opposition to the rampant objectivity of his age is a rejection of factual, objective knowledge. In reality, his complaint is not directed against the facts themselves, and does not question their existence or validity as such. Kierkegaard's denunciation of objectivity focuses instead on those individuals who are so caught up in systems and objectivity and abstract thought that they have forgotten what it means to *exist* (*CUP* 216). Such persons have engaged themselves in the "process of ceasing to be a human being," and are therefore as responsive to the demands of inwardness as a "walking stick" (*CUP* 268). As a result, the majority of human beings live as knives without handles, arrows without tips, wasting their energy and their lives upon the trivial, finite, and mundane things of existence, which renders them "just as unusable for spirit as eyeless sewing needles are for sewing" (*JP* 3:651–52 #3587).[31] Objectivity shields one from personal involvement, and by doing so, *ipso facto* precludes a true God-relationship and an authentic existence. This, in turn, gives rise to the phenomenon of professors who lecture but do not profess, clergy who preach but do not practice, philosophers who speculate but do not relate their contemplations to their own lives, and Christians who talk about Christ but do not emulate him.[32] Symptomatic of this disease of objectivity is the fact that the instructors, professors, and clergymen, from their "objective superior position" of scientific scholarship, categorically exclude a philosopher such as Socrates, for whom philosophy was "merely a life," as well as the early Christians, for whom religion was "only life." According to Kierkegaard, the objective standpoint views as inferior a belief that is synonymous with life, even though, in reality, the separation of belief and existence is an invalidation of both the belief and the existence (*JP* 3:521–22 #3317).[33]

In summary, Kierkegaard employs the concept of subjectivity to express the passionate inwardness of individuals who accept their existence and assume responsibility for their actions. This integrity arises as individuals apply moral and religious injunctions to themselves, instead of merely talking or speculating about them. The individual relates directly only to God, thus becoming increasingly transparent and illuminated under the force of this revelatory relationship. Objectivity, in the sense of an impersonal relationship to the moral and religious imperatives of existence, is the antithesis of this rigorous subjectivity, because it teaches one to conceal oneself in the safety of a crowd of those who share the same impartial opinions, and, in this way, eliminates the necessity of applying moral injunctions to one's own life. This action, however, by frustrating any individual relationship to the self, also precludes any relationship with God. In this sense, Christendom is devoid of Christians and the age is devoid of "real men," because individuals are lacking the passionate inwardness of subjectivity that characterizes a true human being (*JP* 3:651 #3587).

In view of the rigorous and painfully self-conscious concept of subjective existence presented above, one would be justified in wondering which qualities possessed by Lessing would prompt Kierkegaard to present the German thinker as the embodiment of the subjectively existing thinker. It would clearly be anachronistic to impute to the historical Lessing this type of rigorous, self-conscious individuality. The historical situation of the time precluded such a possibility: the Germany of the Enlightenment was a land inured to absolutism. In addition to the fact that they were legally limited in terms of social mobility, the German people were conditioned to accept the dependent status of obedient subjects. For this reason, society at large had not yet achieved the level of social and personal consciousness at which the idea of individuals who had right in themselves merely by force of their existence could be universally conceived.[34] It is true that the ideals of the Enlightenment stressed the individual appropriation of truth and the personal exercise of reason and understanding. However, this individualness is of a markedly collective character. That is: the individual, blocked in social progression, turns inward to focus on the pursuit of personal truth, enlightenment, and understanding. This effort, in turn, demolishes the barriers of personal weakness and confusion of thought, and thus unites the individual with the body of humanity, which is pressing forward toward the higher goal of universal truth and enlightenment.[35]

Lessing's work does, in fact, illustrate this type of collective consciousness and emphatic universality, because it is quite simply void of reference to the individual as such. The concept does not seem to have ever occurred to him. Although he is constantly involved in the discussion and critique of both the thought and the literary production of historical and contemporary individuals, his interest in no sense extends to an evaluation of those individuals in and of themselves. Significantly enough in the context of this discussion, the closest Lessing seems to have come to the valuation of an individual because of his individuality is the brief mention of Socrates in the *Dramaturgy*.[36] In this passage Lessing's praise consists of the observation that the Greek philosopher's mode of life itself was the only morality that he preached. It was, therefore, Socrates' life which made him so valuable, both to those in direct contact with him, such as the tragedian Euripides, and to humankind as a whole. Like Kierkegaard, Lessing was impressed, not with what Socrates said, but rather with what he was.

Except for this instance, any interest that Lessing displays in historical individuals seems to have arisen predominantly from his involvement as a drama critic. In the same sense, his relationship to historical detail, when he considers it at all, is conditioned by the needs of dramatic authorship. His concern is consistently focused on universal truth rather than historical singularity. In relationship to dramatic production he states emphatically:

From the stage we are not to learn what such and such an individual man has done, but what every man of a certain character would do under certain given circumstances. The object of tragedy is more philosophical than the object of history. (*HD* 52)[37]

Lessing maintains this same attitude toward the individual as a historical concretion, in all areas of his writing, including the most personal. In fact, in direct contrast to the easy, conversational openness with which he develops his thought for public view, he preserves almost complete silence concerning the details and facts of his own life, even in his most informal correspondence. When pressed as a young man for specific information concerning himself, he responded with the question:

Can one say anything more important of a person without servants, without friends, without prosperity than his name? As yet I can distinguish myself through little else besides this. (*LS* 17:40 #34)[38]

Lessing's personal correspondence provides, at least to some degree, a chronicle of his *inner* state at various times of his life, particularly in his later years, although it supplies almost no external biographical information. In his public and published works, however, Lessing scrupulously avoids all mention of the personal, whether it be external circumstance or internal feeling. An important clue to the understanding of Lessing's relationship to the personal and individual can be found in the *Dramaturgy*, where Lessing describes a situation in which Voltaire happened to be present in the theater during the production of one of his own plays. Lessing notes that the audience, curious to see the author in person, created an uproar until Voltaire appeared on stage to be viewed and applauded. After admitting that he is not certain whether he is more surprised at the childish curiosity of the public or the vanity of the author, Lessing asks:

How do people think that a poet looks? Not like other mortals? And how weak must be the impression made by his work if in the end one desires nothing more ardently than to see the face of its maker. (*HD* 103)

His conclusion is most significant for this discussion:

The true masterpiece, so it seems to me, fills us so entirely with itself that we forget its author over his work, that we do not regard it as the production of a simple being but as the work of general nature. (Ibid.)

Lessing further asserts that the reason for the lack of information concerning Homer as a person lies in the superb nature of his poetry, then finishes as follows:

> He leads us among gods and heroes and we must feel great *ennui* in this society if we want to look round and inquire after the porter who has admitted us. (Ibid.)[39]

The fact that Lessing perceives the individual in terms of a collective humanity is, therefore, mirrored in his conviction that the work of a given author should be understood as the product of universal nature. The author or particular individual is then, in this sense, only the tool, the doorkeeper who opens the way into the supra-individual realm of universality.

In view of the aforementioned, it would seem almost to be a misstatement when Climacus directly asserts that Lessing "religiously shut himself up within the isolation of his own subjectivity" (*CUP* 61). In reality, Climacus himself is cognizant of the distance that separates his perspective from that which, at least in the external view, seems to have characterized Lessing. And he is not unaware of the historical limitations that impinge on individuals and circumscribe their development. As he admits:

> In connection with this task of becoming essentially subjective, it is necessary to take into account the scope of the reflective presuppositions that the subject has to interpenetrate, the weight of the objectivity he has to throw off; and how infinite a conception he has of the significance of this change (the change from objectivity to subjectivity), its responsibility and its limits. (*CUP* 62)

He also observes that, in achieving a level of essential subjectivity in his God-relationship:

> Lessing has seized upon that Archimedean point of the religious life, which does not precisely enable one to move the world, but which it needs an energy of cosmic proportions to discover, when you have Lessing's presuppositions. (*CUP* 61)

With these statements, Climacus relativizes the position of the historical Lessing by penetrating the presuppositions and historical limitations. He is not interested in the dead weight of mortal actuality; his concern is to expose the lightness of essential ideality. If one is willing to look with Climacus beyond the factual boundaries,

one will, indeed, perceive a certain spirit, a certain essence in the attitudes and actions of the historical Lessing, which finds its correspondence in the figure of the Lessing pseudonym. The concept of
the individual is a case in point. Lessing's age, and Lessing himself,
had not yet learned to break the mass of humanity down into individually existing, intrinsically valuable, and self-directing human beings. And yet it cannot be denied that Lessing's perception of
individuals in society was, in many ways, as radical for his age as
Kierkegaard's individuality was in a later century. Lessing lived at a
juncture in time when the German middle-class was slowly awakening to a consciousness of itself as "other" than the general mass of
existing humanity. It was a time when the *Bürger* (citizen, here implicitly middle-class) was beginning to feel his or her incipient
power and right as a member of a social group, which, in turn, was
learning to define itself over and against the nobility. With his successful introduction of the *Bürgerliches Trauerspiel* (a tragedy with
characters drawn predominantly from the middle-class) into the German theater, with his works such as *Emilia Galotti* and his unabashed
demand that dramatic protagonists be of the same bone and fiber as
the viewers (*LS* 10:104), Lessing was at the forefront of this awakening consciousness. Because the phenomenon of the author who is
actively engaged in the promotion of a particular social cause was
not yet possible within the limitations of the age, Lessing can in no
sense be viewed as an activist involved in the cause of the middle-
class. Nevertheless, he did, indeed, demonstrate a strong sense of
the collective individuality and worth of the *Bürger* as a valuable
part of humanity. And he asserted this belief, particularly in his
dramatic works—not only in the actual plot, as in *Emilia Galotti*, but
also in the fact that he drew his heroes and heroines from the ranks
of Bourgeois society, and he attempted to endow their speech with
the natural flow of everyday conversation.

But even beyond this point of correspondence that unites the pseudonymic and the historical Lessing, it is possible to isolate another
quality that helps to clarify Kierkegaard's choice of Lessing as the
embodiment of the subjectively existing thinker. This trait can be illustrated only in reference to Kierkegaard's conception of Socrates.
In fact, Lessing himself hit on this point when he noted that the legacy which Socrates left to Euripides consisted, not in a body of eloquent moral dicta, but rather in his manner of existence in and of
itself. There is, in fact, within the historical Lessing, a definite congruence of thought and deed, an actualization of philosophy in practice that cannot be overlooked. In this sense, although Lessing was
not necessarily consciously aware of the individual as such, he did, in

fact, embody in his own existence many of the traits that Kierkegaard would later attribute to the passionately existing individual. Like Socrates, that which Lessing believed was "merely his life"; one finds in Lessing very little separation of life from philosophy.[40] The validity of this point will become increasingly clear as this discussion progresses.

In addition to congruence of thought and action, Kierkegaard's previously defined concept of subjectivity also contains a strong element of personal decision and responsibility. As with the notion of the individual, however, it would seem at first that Lessing in actuality exhibited the direct opposite of this concept in his work. For various reasons, it was common practice during the time period in question to publish one's works anonymously. Lessing himself was no stranger to this practice, a fact that Kierkegaard criticized strongly in his later writings. This authorial anonymity not only applies to many of Lessing's reviews, critiques and polemic works—it also extends to several of his more major creative and philosophical works. For example, when discussing the project of *Emilia Galotti*, he refers to himself in the third person as "my young tragedian" (*LS* 17:133 #88). Similarly, he describes the *Erziehung* (Education of the Human Race) as having been written by a good friend (*LS* 18:269 #597), and at another point expressly states that he will never claim it as his own (*LS* 18:335 #674).

This attitude of anonymity could conceivably be construed as a desire to escape responsibility for one's writings, an illustration of the type of flight into the crowd that Kierkegaard condemns so heartily. When considered in light of Lessing's own statements, however, this assumption proves to be unfounded. As has already been pointed out, Lessing believes that the personality and factuality of the author is not only irrelevant to, but also a detraction from the universal nature of a true work of art. His assertion that a real masterwork will be so forceful that its effect will totally eclipse any thought of the author illustrates an attitude of authorial/critical anonymity, which seems to be a characteristic, not only of Lessing's work, but of his age in general. Just as Lessing's subjective consciousness appears to have been more collective than individual, so the authoritative *I* that speaks in his reviews, articles, and critical and polemic works is ostensibly more the voice of a period of critics than the result of a consciousness of the self as an *I* with a personal opinion. The point that lends a sense of subjectivity in terms of personal decision, involvement, and responsibility for one's words and actions is the fact that, within the limitations of this collective authoritative *I*, an opinion or, more exactly, a personal judgement is passed and unabashedly defended as valid. However, this spirit of criticism that runs, as the propelling artistic and philosophical force, through all of Lessing's work is by no means a matter of arbitrary personal judgement. Criticism, by definition, presupposes an absolute or normative standard against which to measure, a fact clearly apparent in Lessing's writings. As Ruth Angress observes:

> Lessing's approach to matters of theory and criticism and the source of his polemic fervor, that quality of style which still has an electrifying effect on his readers today, is due to something that he shares with his own Templar: a conviction that there is such a thing as true and reliable authority if one could just find the right source of it.[41]

For example, Lessing's aesthetic critique is based on a thorough study of the ancients, in conjunction with the observation of actual application in poetic work. To this he adds a knowledge of the works of the few modern writers whom he considers to be masters. With great confidence he is able, therefore, to declare of himself:

> I believe that I have studied the art of dramatic composition; that I have studied it more than twenty who practice it. I, too, have practiced it as much as is necessary to be qualified to put in a word or two. . . .
>
> But one can study and deliberate himself deep into error. That which therefore assures me that the same has not happened to me, that I do not mistake the nature of the art of dramatic composition is this, that I perceive it entirely as Aristotle abstracted it from the innumerable masterpieces of the Greek stage. (*LS* 10:214)

And, just as his aesthetic criticism is grounded on a solid foundation of ancient and modern masters, so Lessing bases his theological argumentation on a deep familiarity both with the Bible and with the writings of the Church Fathers. Once again, with the assurance born of thorough scholarship, he can claim: "The most widely read in this matter had no more sources than I. The most widely read can therefore know no more than I." (*LS* 13:335)[42]

In Lessing's opinion, however, successful artistic production and, as necessarily follows, sound criticism are not merely a matter of factual scholarship. Lessing insists, not only on a study of the canons of morality, but also on a certain level of actualization of these moral tenets in the individual life, as becomes clear in his admonition to his brother Karl:

> Study Morals diligently, learn to express yourself well and correctly, and cultivate your own character: without this, I cannot conceive of any good dramatic writer. (*LS* 17:269 #213)[43]

The fact that Lessing bases his criticism on a solid framework of thorough scholarship combined with the canons of morality is, in and of itself, not sufficient to distinguish him from his contemporaries or make him stand out as particularly unique. Lessing was a critic in an age of critics, and thus inherited the same mind-set, the same types of absolute standards as were employed by others. That which imbues his work with a distinct subjective character is his fearless assertion of his perception of morality, reason, taste, and judgement, and *his* understanding of the rules found in the ancients. This assertion, of course, is made in direct contradiction to others who also believe that their values and judgments are based on the authority of the same masters and ancients which Lessing cites.[44]
Although it never comes to discussion in his works as such, the concept of personal decision and responsibility that plays such an important role in Kierkegaard's concept of subjectivity does occupy a major position in Lessing's mode of criticism. It appears, not only in his propensity to affirm his own viewpoint, but also in the direction and purpose of his criticism. One of Lessing's greatest complaints against individuals such as Johann Christoph Gottsched is that they erroneously attempt to establish and to enforce their own taste as the absolute standard for everyone. In Lessing's opinion, true critics do not attempt to derive the rules of art from their own personal taste; instead, their taste must be drawn from the rules inherent in works of genius (*LS* 9:260 – 61).[45] And, even more important, Lessing sees the critic as one who teaches, enlightens, and persuades, but never as one who is authorized to legislate or dictate. Hans Mayer points out that Lessing never feels his own calling to be that of an aesthetic legislator. To the contrary, he perceives himself to be the aesthetic district attorney (Kronjurist) watching over the correct application of aesthetic rules.[46] In other words:

> The public is conceded its say before the critic, and Lessing conceives of himself as its advocate. In this, however, it should be remembered that even with him, this "right to speak" extends only so far as the expectations of the public coincide with those of the artistic critic Lessing. Lessing considers it to be his responsibility first to shape these expectations, first to rear the public to an enlightened-critical state.[47]

It is this concept of educating the public that brings Lessing closest to Kierkegaard in this regard. Education, to Lessing, is not a matter of prescribing a set of principles that must be accepted as absolute. His method is much closer to the Socratic maieutic, which attempts, above all, to provoke others to think and form judgements for themselves. The reader is required constantly to decide who is right and who is wrong. To summarize in the words of Angress:

> Lessing manages to transform any aesthetic or literary issue into a family dispute where a large clan is shouting and gesticulating and clamoring to be heard. The author is party to the dispute. And the reader, while he is not exactly being asked to change his life . . . is in fact required to do the eighteenth-century equivalent thereof, namely to make up his mind, to choose a side and abandon passivity. He is not required to strike out on his own, only to own up to his intellectual provenance or . . . to profess "whose intellectual child he is."[48]

In addition to the notion of the individual and the demand for personal decision mentioned previously, Kierkegaard's conception of subjectivity is characterized by the necessity for a passionate personal commitment to truth. In this area Lessing unequivocally embodies the impassioned intensity of the subjectively existing individual. Lessing's entire production and, in actuality, his life itself, is governed by an overriding drive toward the truth. Truth, for him, is no absolute to be possessed;[49] rather, it is the object of endless searching, it is a process, not an end point. Like Kierkegaard, Lessing is less profoundly involved in the *what* of truth. That, for him, would fall into the category of possession, which can only make one indolent and proud. The point that endows Lessing's thought with a flexibility almost unknown to the Germany of his time is that he, like Kierkegaard, is most dynamically engaged in the *how* of truth: the manner in which it is pursued and presented, the way in which it is lived. In his opinion:

> A man who, with good intentions, attempts as shrewdly as unpretentiously to carry falsehood through against opposing conviction, is of endlessly more worth than a man who defends the best, most noble truth through prejudice, in a routine way, by decrying his opponents. (*LS* 13:23)

Lessing's commitment to truth is the force that transforms practically the entire body of his published and private works into an ongoing battle against pedantry and inflexibility in all spheres. In his view, the dogged insistence on the letter of the rule, which characterizes much of the thought during his age, presents a real obstacle to the pursuit of truth, because it tends to smother the questioning, questing spirit that is the moving power of intellectual life and growth. In a sense, Lessing's attack on the pedantry of his intellectual peers is comparable, within the presuppositions of his age, to the offensive that Kierkegaard launched against the prevalent objectivity of his period.

Within the aesthetic sphere, for example, Lessing published works such as the *Literaturbriefe* (Letters on Literature), the *Dramaturgy,* and *Laokoon* in an attempt to point out and counteract the tastelessness, mediocrity, and wholesale imitation of French styles then rampant in Germany. However, his is not a destructive progressiveness that desires to break down the old ways at all costs. He is quite aware of the value of even mediocre works in filling up the literary and artistic void that plagued the Germany of his time, and in preparing public taste to receive works of greater genius. And yet he never hesitates to judge a piece for what it is. In his words: "When the lame race one another, the one of them who reaches the goal first still remains a lame man" (*LS* 9:211).[50] He attacks the stiff, unnatural pompousness of literary language, demanding in its place an unaffected, living flow. As a young man he advised his sister, "Write as you speak, and then you will write beautifully" (*LS* 17:3 #1). This call for naturalness persists throughout his entire career: Everything within a dramatic character must spring from natural causes, the language of heart and feeling must not be destroyed by pedantic insistence on cold grammatical logic, the lines spoken by actors must arise from within, rather than appearing to be mechanically learned, servants should speak as servants, queens should speak as human beings.[51] The list could be continued *ad infinitum.* But the common denominator among all these artistic demands is the desire for an aesthetic presentation that is congruent with that which is highest in human existence. Also, Lessing not only challenges other writers to achieve these levels of artistic naturalness, but he also seeks to reduplicate them in his own work. That he succeeds to a large degree, is confirmed by the fact that his works not only are still read, but also are performed on modern stages, whereas the attempts of most of his contemporaries have long since vanished into literary oblivion. Structurally his dramas are characterized by a quick, relatively easy flow of dialogue, a flexible relationship to the Aristotelian rules of drama, and a natural progression of action, which, at times, borders on the improvisatory.[52] This same drive to transcend the confines of pedantic narrowness and shortsightedness is also illustrated in Lessing's dramas on a philosophical and psychological level. The plot in even his earliest dramatic works arises directly from the conflict between unyielding rigidity of attitude and various levels of more pliable and "enlightened" understanding. The comedies depict the foolishness of such limited attitudes; in the tragedies, this same inflexibility of mind proves fatal. In *Minna von Barnhelm*, for example, the entire plot revolves around Minna's personal struggle to awaken Tellheim from his self-destructive concept of honor. Similarly, in the dramatic poem *Nathan der Weise* (Nathan the Wise), the title character is surrounded by the limited and unyielding attitudes of Daja, the young crusader, the Sultan, the Patriarch, and the often overly enthusiastic Recha.

Lessing's insistence on flexibility and openness in the search for truth stands out even more strikingly within the realm of theology. As in the aesthetic sphere, he is once again no revolutionary—he is aware of the danger in pouring off the dirty water before he has found liquid from a purer source to replace it (*LS* 18:101–02 #404). But this innate sense of caution does not deter him in any way from the fearless denunciation of falsehood and spiritual rigor mortis that he perceives in the theological world. Without hesitation he condemns the fashionable shallowness of the Neologists, who waver somewhere in the twilight between theology and philosophy. The disgruntled founders of various Christian sects also fall under heavy criticism because, in Lessing's view, it is not error itself, but rather error that is codified into a denominational belief which is the source of human unhappiness. Lessing admits a degree of sympathy toward the more tolerant traditional theology, since the Orthodoxy is at least honest enough to fight openly against human understanding rather than secretly attempting to bribe it.[53] And yet Lessing does not at any time consider the Orthodoxy to be other than an enemy to the search for truth, and he feels it to be his task to expose the complacency and destructive numbness at any cost, even though the entire religious world should be shaken to the point that a few believers are lost. As he emphatically declares:

I do not wish intentionally to crush any worm underfoot; but if it is to be accounted to me as sin if I crush one by chance: then I do not know how else to counsel myself, except that I do not move at all; that I bring none of my limbs out of the position in which it is once found; that I cease living. Every movement in the physical realm generates and destroys, brings life and death; brings this creature death, in that it brings that one life: would it be better to have no death, and no movement? or preferably, death and motion? (*LS* 13:165)

In equally strong terms, he denounces what he views to be the hypocritical desire of the Orthodoxy to ban the storm wind from nature, in spite of the good it might do. As he avers, their complaint originates, not in their concern for the ship which occasionally might be driven up onto a sandbank, but rather in their fear that their own private gardens might be disturbed by the wind's passage.[54]

Significant particularly to this discussion is the fact that Lessing repeatedly refers to the publication of the Samuel Reimarus fragments, which initiated his most intense and prolonged theological debate, as an attempt to gain personal peace and understanding in relationship to the doubts raised by his reading of the Reimarus manuscript. The question he tosses out to Pastor Goeze rings as a clear challenge:

> Am I nothing to myself? Have I no duty towards myself, to seek reassurance where I believe I will find it? . . . I know very well that an individual is obligated to sacrifice his personal temporal welfare for the welfare of the many. But also his eternal welfare? What before God and man can bind me, preferably not to desire to free myself from tormenting doubts, rather than to annoy those of feeble faith by disclosing them? (*LS* 13:184)[55]

This statement not only illustrates Lessing's intense commitment to the search for truth; it also asserts the right and responsibility of the individual to find satisfaction concerning the truth. That Lessing should make such a statement was a bold step. That he should assert it publicly was an act of affrontive daring, in light of the restrictions of his age.

This subjective element of impassioned involvement in the quest for truth, with its corollary offensive against rigidity and intolerance is clearly evident throughout Lessing's work on the human level as well. Although he is not in a position to express the validity of the individual *qua* individual, he does, indeed, strongly assert the validity of human beings as an integral and valuable part of humanity.

The concept of flexible and tolerant humanity can be isolated first of all in the aesthetic structure of Lessing's dramas. It becomes immediately evident, particularly in his mature works, that Lessing endeavors above all to endow his dramatic characters with a true and rounded humanity. With the exception, perhaps, of the Patriarch in *Nathan*, who represents the petrified institution of the Church rather than a human being as such, Lessing's personages are no mannered caricatures of absolute evil or absolute good. It is Lessing's conviction that dramatic characters, like human beings, must exhibit a mixture of good and evil, strength and weakness (*LS* 8:167; 10:97).

Whether it be the interplay of hate, remorse, revenge, and forgiveness in *Miß Sara Sampson*, the battle between unprincipled desire and virtue's fear for its own weakness in *Emilia Galotti*, or the conflict between head and heart in *Minna*, Lessing's dramas deal with the conflicts and emotions of human beings—not idealized heroes or majestic rulers, but beings of the same bone and fiber as the viewers themselves. In the same sense, Lessing's tragedies are not determined by either fate or a particular heroic flaw. Rather, the outcome is shaped by the clash of human beings with flawed humanity, which drives the guilty, the confused and the innocent into a situation from which there is no return.

In addition to this architectural embodiment of the call for a revised attitude toward humanity, Lessing also presents a direct and vivid statement in the actual story lines of his dramas, from early attempts such as *Der Misogyn* (The Misogyn) and *Die Juden* (The Jews) to the culmination in *Nathan*. The immense significance of *Nathan*, for example, arises not only from the fact that the protagonist is a Jew, but also in the point that this Jew is uniquely humane, the literal personification of Enlightenment ideals. That the Christians appear as the least tolerant of all characters is far from inconsequential, while the final revelation of the blood relationship between the Christians and the Moslems solidifies an assertion of the universal interdependence of humankind that far outstrips the author's historical period.

This drive against inflexibility and frozen attitudes in the human sphere is not limited, by any means, to Lessing's dramatic works. It receives its most direct formulation in *Ernst und Falk* (Ernst and Falk). From a basically political point of view, the freemason diagnoses the interhuman conflict in the world as the result of the divisions among nations and peoples, which are both precipitated and encouraged by the varying purposes of states. As he explains:

> That is: at present, when a German meets a Frenchman, a Frenchman an Englishman or vice versa, no longer does a mere human being meet a mere human being, who is drawn to the other on the strength of their similar natures, but rather, one such human being meets another particular human being, both of whom are conscious of their differing tendencies, which makes them cold, distant, suspicious of one another. (*LS* 13:356)

In terms of Kierkegaard's conception of subjectivity, with its demand for congruence of belief and action, it is of particular importance that Lessing not only writes concerning this type of human tolerance, but he also lives it. Whether it be his friendship with

Moses Mendelssohn, his defense of women against a prejudice all too easily applied, or his aversion to the overzealous patriotism portrayed by Johann Gleim's *Grenadier*, there seems to be no separation between that which he espouses in writing and that which he practices in actual existence.[56]

In connection with the claim that Lessing's entire thought and existence are involved in an impassioned personal battle against inflexibility and frozen norms, it would be well to consider briefly his attitude toward genius. It is a historical fact that, on the brink of the age of the Romantic Individual, Lessing rejected the work of the young poets and authors who later carried the age into the Storm and Stress movement. The tendency would be to view in this repudiation of the younger generation a manifestation of rational Enlightenment shortsightedness. Although it would be rather narrow to claim that Lessing at no time fell prey to a certain human rigidity of philosophy, it is still important to point out that, as a general rule, Lessing rejected these preromantic works, not because of their new, individualistic traits, but because the writers seemed determined to progress by destroying the established standards of taste and artistic balance, rather than by artistically transcending the limitations of the time. As has been demonstrated, Lessing bases his criticism and artistic production on a firm foundation of the rules of art as they are drawn from the works of ancient masters. His complaint is, therefore, directed at those writers who claim the right to arbitrarily ignore canons of taste and quality in art. As he insists:

> "Genius! Genius!" they shout. "Genius overrides all rules! What genius does is the rule! . . . Rules suppress genius!"—As if genius would allow itself to be suppressed by anything in the world! [Genius] has the pattern of all rules in itself. (*LS* 10:190)

The fact that Lessing is not shackled to the concept of rules merely for the sake of rules is amply illustrated by his constant ridicule of those—particularly the French and their imitators—who push the concept of artistic rule to the point of pedantic absurdity.[57] On the other hand, he also admits:

> Sometime I would really . . . like to shame the frivolous artists, who always boast about their infallible taste, and despise all ancient erudition, which one draws from books. (*LS* 18:61 #372)

The key to this apparent contradiction lies in Lessing's conviction that genius arises naturally from the innate comprehension of rules which it carries within itself. It does not originate in mechanical principles applied from the outside. The fact that Lessing is not tied into inflexible adherence to artistic maxims becomes clear in his assertion that rules are derived from the observation of the manner in which genius creates; these formative principles are then universalized into standards of artistic creation. As he states, "These observations . . . still multiply, whenever a genius, who never entirely follows his predecessors, pursues a new course or opens up the already familiar one beyond the old borders" (*LS* 4:413). It is as much a mistake for critics to apply their standards of measurement to a work, regardless of the spirit of genius, as it is for a genius to attempt to create without the guiding framework of artistic priciples (*LS* 9:322). Only by studying the ways in which other masters have transcended the canons of accepted taste can one learn when and how it is possible to successfully make an exception to the established rule (*LS* 8:145).[58] Within Lessing's conception of genius, there is, in fact, a certain ambivalence apparent in his juxtaposition of the letter of mechanical rules to the spirit of genius. Whereas his scholarly mind-set demands the first, his drive for flexibility and naturalness affirms the other. Perhaps his attitude in this connection can best be described as a healthy and yet affirmative distrust, as this statement of his attitude to Friedrich Gottlieb Klopstock illustrates:

> I assure [you] . . . that I am in all earnestness favorably inclined toward Mr. Klopstock; as I am favorably inclined toward all geniuses. But, just because I recognize him to be a great genius, must I always believe he is right? Absolutely not. Rather, exactly the opposite: because I adjudge him to be a great genius, I am on my guard towards him. I know that a fiery horse can break his neck, along with that of his rider, on exactly that stile, over which the cautious donkey goes without stumbling. (*LS* 8:261–62)

In addition to the points already considered, there is yet another area in Lessing's production in which, following Kierkegaard's definition, an unmistakable subjective quality can be discerned. This is the impassioned and intensely personal tone of Lessing's prose. Particularly in his polemic works, Lessing's style is electric with what Kierkegaard would call a passionate intensity. Whether one reads a personal letter, a polemic argument or an aesthetic treatise, one always gains the impression that there is an intense personal involvement on the part of the author in what has been written. Lessing's consistent choice of imagery drawn from battle within his ongoing literary involvement cannot be overlooked in this context. By definition, "battle" excludes passive noninvolvement. That is, conflict in this sense presupposes both individual commitment and personal risk.[59] Lessing is consciously involved in the Enlightenment campaign against confusion and error and, as he himself observes: "Such things must be said a bit vehemently or it does not help at all" (*LS* 17:258 #203). Among the prime characteristics of his writing are "Offenherzigkeit" (frankness) and "Wahrheit mit Wärme gesagt" (truth spoken with warmth) (*LS* 13:189).[60] It is precisely this manner of speaking what he perceives to be the truth, with candor and animated, vibrant warmth, which infuses into Lessing's works a personal, subjective quality. In fact, the sense of high-powered energy that makes Lessing's works stand in such sharp contrast to other, more prosaic writers of his day is the direct product of the impassioned intensity and absolute focus which are so basic to Lessing's style.

The God-Relationship

No exposition of subjectivity in Kierkegaard's authorship can be isolated from religious implications, since, as the Danish thinker asserts, the question underlying all his thought is, "How do I become a true Christian?" For this reason, although the historical Lessing is active in various fields of inquiry, Kierkegaard's Lessing pseudonym is presented exclusively in conjunction with the religious sphere.

Lessing's "true" religious beliefs have probably been analyzed at greater length and with less critical unity than any other aspect of his thought and production. Climacus, however, holds himself entirely aloof from the critical arena. In actuality, the multiplicity of arguments as to whether Lessing espoused or undermined the Lutheran faith, whether he leaned more toward Catholicism, whether he was predominantly a pantheist or a spinozist have no bearing on the Lessing pseudonym. It is not doctrine that Climacus desires to present, a fact which is underscored by his assertion that Lessing:

> did not permit himself to be deceived into becoming world-historic and systematic with respect to the religious, but understood and knew how to hold fast to the understanding that the religious concerned Lessing, and Lessing alone, just as it concerns every other human being in the same manner; understood that he had infinitely to do with God, and nothing, nothing to do with any man directly. (*CUP* 61)

For Kierkegaard, the heart of Christianity is the God-relationship, a divine affiliation so extraordinary and precious that it can only be approached individually (*CUP* 62–63). Since religion for him is a passionately active inward experience, dogma, which would fall into the category of the passive, the world-historical, the objective and systematic must be left behind as one approaches deity.

Since the Lessing pseudonym embodies the subjective relationship with God, it is of interest that, outside of the theological debates, the historical Lessing rarely speaks of God at all. When he does refer to divine intervention in his life, it is usually through the euphemism "Providence" (*Vorsicht* or *Vorsehung*).[61] One might, for this reason, be inclined to assert that a person who does not speak of God demonstrates very little depth of relationship to divinity. However, as has been previously mentioned, one of the most basic concepts of Kierkegaardian philosophy is the incommunicability of subjective interiority, particularly when it concerns individual God-experience. In this sense, therefore, it is silence that testifies most eloquently of a profound subjective relationship with the divine.[62] Lessing himself is, in actuality, not too far removed from this concept when, in criticizing Martin Wieland, he exclaims: "For Mr. Wieland, the Christian religion is every third word. One often boasts of that which one does not possess at all, so that one at least seems to have it" (*LS* 8:26). To the end of his life, Lessing insisted that he had always been of service to the Christian religion, and that he had specifically defended the Lutheran church against various sects and heretical beliefs.[63] And yet, as is clearly manifest in the "Ring Parable" in *Nathan*, in the parable of the "Burning Palace," and also in the *Erziehung* (Education of the Human Race), Lessing is at no time the exponent of a particular denominational creed. To the contrary, his writings demonstrate the fact that in the religious sphere, as in all other areas, his beliefs are guided by his overriding desire for truth. As he exclaims in this connection: "I hunger so much for conviction, that I, like Erisichthon, devour anything that even resembles nourishment" (*LS* 13:3). It is because of this drive for truth, in conjunction with his desire to encourage in human beings the exercise of rational understanding that he opposes all sects, philosophies, and dogmatic systems that limit individuals by binding them to a predetermined set of beliefs so laden with tradition and sophistic interpolation that they contain more falsehood than truth.[64] By publicizing doubts and heretical statements so that they can be publicly refuted, Lessing feels that he is best serving the cause of truth, even though he faces the risk of falling into error along the way. It is, in fact, his conviction that God has as great a hand in human error as in human truth.[65]

In almost the same sense as Kierkegaard, Lessing is concerned with the actualization of religious belief in daily existence. As a young man he contrasts the passive and unconverted *Scheinchrist* (hypocrite) with the doubter in these terms:

> Time will show whether he is a better Christian, who has the principles of the Christian doctrine in his recollection and often, without understanding them, in his mouth, who goes to church and participates in all rites because they are customary; or he, who at one time has prudently doubted, and has arrived at conviction through the path of inquiry, or who at least has endeavored to gain it. (*LS* 17: 17–18 #12)

His further statement underscores his belief that religion must be a matter of personal involvement rather than indifferent acceptance: "The Christian religion is not an enterprise that one should accept in loyalty and faith, from one's parents" (Ibid., 18). As he laconically observes, most Christians seem to inherit their religion from their parents, just as they inherit money—that is, with no involvement or effort on their part. This circumstance is, in turn, mirrored in the fact that these Christians fail to observe in their actions basic commandments such as love for one's enemies (Ibid.).

Perhaps, as a result of this belief in personal religious involvement rather than dogma, Lessing consistently remains aloof from the judgements of other people concerning his theological deportment. Here Climacus' assertion that Lessing understood that he had infinitely to do with God and nothing to do with any human being directly, finds its greatest congruency with the historical concretion. In the face of Goeze's accusations, Lessing declares that he feels no need to tremble before his hour of death, and expresses his truth-seeking relationship with God as follows:

> Enough, that my heart does not damn me, and I may therefore, with all willingness before God, rip the mask from the face of every intolerant hypocrite who approaches me,—and I will tear it off,—even if the entire hide comes off with it. (*LS* 13:155)[66]

In a simple and yet eloquent statement, made once again to Goeze, Lessing implicitly declares an awareness that he is responsible only to God for his conduct in the Reimarus controversy. After observing that the world pays more attention to what one *appears* to be (Schein) than to what one *is* (Sein), Lessing responds to Goeze's attack on his character in this manner: "with Essence [Sein] there is no problem. That I am not that [which Goeze alleges], only One needs to know.

He knows it." (*LS* 13:34). Perhaps the most comprehensive expression of Lessing's individual relationship to God can be found in the following passage from the *Duplik* (Defendant's Rejoinder):

> If, however, I have not utilized my leisure . . . in the best way: what does it matter? Who knows whether I might not have occupied it even worse with some other endeavor? My intention at least was to use it well. It was my conviction at least, that I could use it well in this way. I will entrust to time, what my candidly spoken opinion should and can effect.—Perhaps it will not effect as much as it could have. . . . If that is the case: then, Thou eternal fountain of all truth, which alone knows if and where it should gush forth, forgive a uselessly industrious servant! He wanted to clear mire out of Thy way. If he has ignorantly thrown away gold nuggets as well: Thy gold nuggets are nevertheless not lost. (*LS* 13:88–89)

Discipleship

The significance of Climacus' insistence that Lessing insures himself against fellowship and prevents discipleship can only be understood in reference to the concepts of subjectivity and the God-relationship previously presented. As has been mentioned, true religion for Kierkegaard arises from the subjective relationship established between the single individual and God. This experience of inner deepening and inwardness in connection with deity should neither be communicated directly nor taught to anyone else. Christianity is not a matter for lecture and speculation—it must be *lived* by each individual. For this reason the notion of the disciple is particularly repugnant to Kierkegaardian philosophy. In Kierkegaard's opinion, a disciple is a person who unquestioningly accepts what someone else has said and repeats it by rote *ad infinitum* without ever appropriating it individually into existence. Disciples tend to admire rather than imitate; they repeat opinions rather than thinking through the situations of existence and drawing the conclusions valid for the individual life.[67] Clearly this rejection of discipleship inherently contains a large element of criticism directed at the Hegelian school, which in Kierkegaard's view had reduced all of existence to a system that thoughtless adherents did indeed repeat by rote, with no concern as to whether or not their existence was at all transformed by the concepts espoused.[68]

In actuality, a relatively large portion of the Lessing description presented by Climacus is specifically concerned with the idea of discipleship. The importance of this concept to Kierkegaard/Climacus is underscored by Climacus' claim that Lessing's merit consists precisely in the fact that he made it impossible for anyone to establish a direct relationship to him through admiration. Climacus particularly remarks on Lessing's:

> adroitness in teasingly using his own ego, almost like Socrates, excusing himself from all fellowship; or rather, insuring himself against fellowship in relation to all that truth, whose chief feature it is, that one must be alone about it. (*CUP* 65)

As Climacus observes, Lessing made no attempt to gather others around him for the sake of triumph since, in relation to the infinite, there is no triumph to win except that of becoming nothing before God. In the same sense, Lessing did not wish to have others with him when he was struggling through the perils of solitary thought, because this solitariness is the way itself. Lessing, in his opinion, not only evaded the efforts of "fanatics" who desired to enroll him in the service of their own social ends, but also eluded their attempts to exclude him (Ibid.). Climacus concludes:

> Even if I strove with might and main to become Lessing's disciple, I could not, for Lessing has prevented it. Just as he himself is free, so I imagine that he desires to make everyone else free in relation to himself. He begs to be excused the exhalations and *gaucheries* of the disciple, fearing to be made ridiculous through repetitioners who reproduce what is said like a prattling echo (Ibid., 67).

Throughout the passages just cited, Climacus implies in Lessing a highly developed level of conscious decision, through his employment of such active verbs as "prevents," "insures," "makes it impossible," "does not wish," and "begs to be excused." However, an examination of the work of the historical Lessing would seem to show, not so much that the author actively insures himself against disciples, but rather that what he is, in combination with the quality of his search for truth, serves *ipso facto* to rebuff others. To apply the type of battle imagery that Lessing himself preferred, it is almost as if he were running out at the head of the vanguard, so caught up in the momentum of the charge that he does not pause to look around or to find out whether or not someone else is running along with him.
The prime historical element that serves automatically to exclude

the possibility of discipleship in the Kierkegaardian sense is the inexorable drive toward freedom which characterizes both Lessing's thought and his personal mode of existence. In the concrete physical sense, this need for freedom expresses itself most vividly in Lessing's consistent refusal to seek any sort of bureaucratic position. This resistance to the accepted societal pattern was not perilous solely in the economic sense. It was also radical almost to the point of being revolutionary at a time when all segments of society accepted as indisputable the fact that the primary avenue to prosperity and security open to the bourgeoisie lay in the procurement of a position under the protection and in the good graces of the nobility. In answer to his father's ceaseless insistence that he arrange for himself what was then called "ein fixiertes Glück," (prosperity through an official appointment) Lessing maintained the right to live independently, from the proceeds of his writing. As he states, "as long as I can still live from my work, and can live in passable comfort, I have not the slightest desire to become the slave of an official post" (*LS* 17:175 #126). At another point he clarifies: "Comfortably means to me that which another would perhaps call want. But what does it matter to me, whether I live in abundance or not, as long as I live" (*LS* 17:21 #14). As a young man he affirmed staunchly that a person who is healthy and unafraid to work has nothing to fear in the world. In his opinion, to worry about the possibility of future incapacitation would be to betray poor faith in Providence (*LS* 17:208 #157). His response to the suggestion that he actively apply for bureaucratic office is emphatic: "To offer my services? I would go with more enthusiasm into death" (*LS* 18:107 #407).[69] As history shows, this life as an independent journalist was plagued from the first by debt and financial restriction. The more mature—and less optimistic—Lessing repeatedly advised his brother not to follow his example, but rather to seek a position that would insure him financial security. In the later years of his life, Lessing exclaimed with some bitterness, "The tame horse is fed in the stall, and must serve: the wild one in his wilderness is free, goes to ruin however in hunger and misery" (*LS* 18:108 #408). And yet, in spite of the ongoing financial difficulties, it is significant to note that the only time Lessing lost his buoyant faith in Providence and succumbed to despair and frustration was when he bowed to society and financial pressure and accepted an official position. Even during the relatively short term in Breslau, his letters reflect confusion, boredom and difficulty in producing creative work. This tendency became far more pronounced during his tenure at Wolfenbüttel. As a general rule, the letters from this period constantly register illness, "hypochondria," irritability and depression. Often,

Lessing reports stretches in which he is unable to involve himself in any sort of literary endeavor at all. It was his abiding desire to leave that position as quickly as possible, although, as it happened, circumstances and financial straits did not allow him to fulfill his hope of regaining his former independent status.[70]

A second manifestation of Lessing's urge for freedom is his innate refusal to be bound by limitations of nation, custom, and false manners. His cosmopolitan attitude toward patriotism and his universally humanitarian works such as *Nathan* and *Ernst und Falk* (Ernst and Falk) have already been mentioned. But in his personal relationship to society at court he showed himself no more willing—or able—to comfortably accommodate his individuality to the accepted norm. In his opinion, the manners displayed in aristocratic circles convert human beings into machines. Of his own participation in this activity, he notes:

> [I] have done with others that which certainly does not help anything if one does it, but which can well be detrimental if one continually neglects it: I have made obeisance and flapped my jaws. (*LS* 18:71 #378)

To Eva König he reports on an occasion that demanded that he pay his respects to the Duchess of Weimar, with the comment: "Is it not true that you must laugh when you think of me and paying court at the same time? Of course I approach it as if I were driven with a whip to do it" (*LS* 17:384 #301). The basic freedom of his nature made it very difficult for him to affect manners which were not natural to him. As he explains:

> I am so little in the habit of being on my guard; I am so little concerned about always showing only my good side, and even my good side is so cross-eyed, that I must be quite content if only others do not entirely despise me in the first moments. (*LS* 17:308 #249)

In fact, in conjunction with the points just illustrated, it can be observed that a certain restlessness and need for change emerge as integral to Lessing's personality. This type of native discontentment comes to expression, for example, when Lessing, who is contemplating a journey to Italy, remarks: "I do not think that Rome would be any more to my liking than any place in the world has ever been" (*LS* 17:271 #216). From Wolfenbüttel he writes: "my present isolation is great, and would be intolerable to one who did not love all change from black to white as much as I do" (*LS* 17:322 #261). The most striking instance of this restlessness appears in Lessing's sudden flight from Berlin to Breslau, the reason for which he describes through the medium of a conversation with himself:

> "Fool!" I say, and strike myself on the brow: "when will you begin to be content with yourself? It is quite true that nothing really drove you from Berlin. . . . But was not everything your free will? Were you not sick and tired of Berlin? Did you not believe that your friends must be fed up with you? that it was truly time once again to live more among human beings than among books?" (*LS* 17:179 #130)

Of even greater importance to the assertion that Lessing insured himself against discipleship is the fact that these same qualities of discontent, unrest and the need for freedom are manifest in equal strength in his intellectual existence. Once again, it would be anachronistic to assert that Lessing consciously attempted to prevent others from adopting his way of thinking. Indeed, he seems not to have considered the concept of personal followers or a "Lessingian" school of thought at all. That he was opposed to this type of endeavor is reflected in the fact that some of his most scathing criticism is reserved for those who attempt to codify their personal taste into universal law, and those more concerned with rearing dependent followers than reasoning human beings.[71] Perhaps the best description of Lessing's own opinion of his work in relationship to the public can be found in this passage from the introduction to the *Erziehung* (Education of the Human Race):

> In it, the author has placed himself on a hill, from which he believes he can survey something more than the prescribed path of his present day. But he calls no eagerly hasty wanderer from his path, who only wishes soon to reach his lodging for the night. He does not require that the view which delights him must also charm all other eyes. (*LS* 13:415)

That is, guided by his own polemic quest for truth, Lessing through his writing seems to have desired more to convince readers of the error and falsehood in the publications of others than specifically to bind them to his particular point of view. The fact that Lessing attempts to provoke others to reason for themselves is in itself a deterrent to any who might seek thoughtlessly to absorb his work as their own. Lessing himself demonstrates an awareness of this fact when he states:

> When a daring spirit, full of trust in his own strength, forces his way into the temple of Taste through a new entrance, there are a hundred imitative

spirits directly behind him, who hope to steal in through this opening along with him. But in vain; with precisely that strength, with which he forced the gate, he slams it closed behind him. His astonished retinue sees itself locked out, and suddenly the immortality of which they were dreaming is transformed into derisive laughter. (*LS* 4:399–400)[72]

Therefore, as will be discussed in greater detail at a later point, the elasticity and restless openness of Lessing's search for truth serves almost automatically to close the door on any who might desire to follow him as a disciple or devotee. The search is too internally directed, too individual, too free-flowing. Lessing once observed, "A wanderer is easily found: but a stroller is difficult to locate" (*LS* 18:333 #671). And, in actuality, the unbounded form of Lessing's thought contains far more resemblance to the work of a *Spaziergänger* (stroller) than to that of a systematic philosopher, a fact which *eo ipso* makes his production unapproachable to those who are interested merely in following.

For Lessing, truth is open-ended; in his opinion, the hunt is far preferable to the catch,[73] and for this reason both his personal existence and his writings are rich with the desire, not only to learn, but also to be taught by others. As he emphatically states: "I do not wish to excuse myself; I wish to better myself" (*LS* 18:331 #670); and again, "I gladly put up with a small humiliation for the sake of a great lesson" (*LS* 13:109). In the same sense, his constant invitation to polemic opponents is "Teach me a better concept of this subject if I am wrong."[74] Perhaps the sense of challenge that Lessing exhibits in regards to the pursuit of truth comes to clearest expression when he writes to a friend:

> I believe just as little as you do, that up until now we have come much further in our dispute than just over the first borders. But do you really have as much inclination as I have, to venture further in and discover this unknown land, even if we should go astray a hundred times along the way? (*LS* 17:89–90 #59)[75]

Such an attitude automatically precludes followers, because it leaves them nothing concrete to grasp and espouse. However, in light of Climacus' claims, it must be emphasized that this situation arises naturally, as a by-product of Lessing's personal manner of procedure, rather than as the result of conscious philosophical conviction.

Interestingly enough, in addition to the points already discussed, Lessing's own attitude toward his work presents a deterrent to any potential adherents, in that he habitually minimizes the value and quality of his work. Among his most frequently applied labels, one finds descriptive terms such as "Katzbalgerei" (scuffling, *LS* 13:336); "Torheiten" (folly, *LS* 17:418 #327); "kritische Alfanzereien" (critical silliness, *LS* 17:399 #313); "Possen" (pranks, *LS* 17:373 #295 and 18:286 #611); "Quark" (balderdash, *LS* 17:285 #227); "Reimereien" (bad rhymes, *LS* 17:213 #160); "Lappalien" (trifles, *LS* 17:171 #123); "theologische Scharmützel" (theological skirmishes, *LS* 18:260 #585); "Sudeleien" (scribbling, *LS* 18:101 #404); "elende Bibliothekarische Kahlmäusereien," (a librarian's miserable petty thievery, *LS* 18:62 #373); and, frequently, "Bettel" (rubbish, *LS* 17:349 #279; 17:346 #276; and 17:264 #210). *Laokoon*, in his description, is a "Mischmasch von Pedanterie und Grillen," (hodgepodge of pedantry and fancy, *LS* 17:222 #172); *Nathan* merely a "Ding von einer Tragödie," (a thing of a tragedy, *LS* 18:18 #345); the theological debate a "Steckenpferd" (hobby, *LS* 18:284–85 #610). Such references serve automatically to create distance, and, therefore, an effective alienating obstacle between the author Lessing and the recipients of his work.

In the same sense, Lessing most often deflated and devaluated the praise that others attempted to shower on him. Representative of this fact is the almost painful self-debate with which Lessing responds to Wieland's praise of *Emilia Galotti*:

this man assures me of his approbation of one of my works, which I would not wish should remain my best, in such a manner—in such a manner! It cannot be irony. How should I answer this man? A complete rejection of his praise would be an affront. Reciprocal praise would be just as great an offense; and more insipid. . . . If he now in a cold, dispassionate hour . . . does not regret his letter: what a dangerous enticement for me! If the most perfect reader whom I can think of is content with it: then good—But he should not fear that I will misuse his praise. I will not forget that the most perfect reader is at the same time the most warm-hearted. That which he himself reads into it makes him warmer than that which he reads. (*LS* 18:53 #368)[76]

Such resistance to praise occurs far too frequently, and too earnestly to be a mere display of fashionable artistic modesty. A large part of this attitude seems to arise directly from Lessing's innate compulsion to learning and progression, and the attendant interest in the tool most suited to stimulate that type of growth: honest criticism. He is convinced that, whereas praise makes one proud and idle, friendly criticism incites one to do better. Characteristically, therefore, one finds Lessing thanking a friend for his approbation, and then without hesitation adding:

> —But now, the better type of acclaim, which we can give one another, just between us: your criticism! . . . Criticism, I will confide in you, is the only method of renewing me so I can do more, or rather, of inciting me to more. (*LS* 18:32 #356)[77]

The fact that he also views criticism as an invaluable aid to learning becomes apparent in this statement to Moses Mendelssohn:

> I want to have my thoughts scrutinized by you, not praised. I look forward to your further objections with that pleasure with which one must look forward to correction. (*LS* 17:75 #55)[78]

Thus, through his demand for and, incidentally, delivery of criticism and debate in the place of praise and admiration, Lessing once again establishes an alienating distance between himself and any potential devotee.

A further characteristic that tends to isolate Lessing is the fact that, particularly in his later years, he tends to avoid involvement in group or joint efforts. For example, he turned his back on continued attempts to enlist his aid in the founding of a German theater, on the grounds that the absence of a German national identity made such a venture premature.[79] He likewise refused to become involved in Friedrich Nicolai's proposed publication of speeches and poetry on the occasion of Ewald von Kleist's death, because, in his opinion, the undertaking betrayed a reprehensible lack of taste and feeling (*LS* 17:170 #122). When Martin Wieland invited him to assist with the *Merkur*, Lessing responded unequivocally: "What sort of contributions do you expect from me? Works of genius? All genius has now been confiscated by certain people, with whom I would not like to find myself on the same path" (*LS* 18:129 #429).

In addition to this avoidance of popular causes, Lessing also made a frequent practice of defying public opinion and defending the weaker cause, even if it did not correspond to his own views. His publication of *Rettungen*[80] of various writers from Plautus to Berengarius Tuonensius attests amply to this fact. As Lessing himself states: "In respect to the ancient writers, I am a true knight errant; my blood immediately boils when I see that they are so deplorably maltreated" (*LS* 17:133–34 #88). And again, "He whom everyone beats to a pulp is safe from me" (*LS* 18:72 #378).[81]

Section II: Lessing's Silence

Lessing, through his silence and calculated withdrawal into himself offers no results, develops no system, and presents nothing which thoughtless adherents could repeat by rote.

This statement will be analyzed in two segments: (1) the concept of silence, and (2) the lack of system.

Silence

The overriding question that gives direction to Kierkegaard's authorship is "How can I become a Christian?" and at the very heart of his exploration of this question lies his concept of communication. As he believes, in order to become truly Christian, one must establish a direct God-relationship. That is, one must learn to exist as an individual before God, which relationship results in an ever-deepening inwardness, an interiority of religious experience.

But this true religiousness and spiritual interiority is something that must be kept silent because, in Kierkegaard's view, "Silence is the way of interiorization for us ordinary human beings" (*JP* 4:99 #3981). This silence is a way of concentration on one's divine origin—"There must, after all, be something which is so holy that it cannot be expressed in words—otherwise how did those men to whom something absolutely tremendous was revealed become: dumb?" (*JP* 1:252 #617). Since it is the task of individuals to relate solely to God in reference to matters of greatest importance, as soon as one turns to other human beings, this affiliation is weakened. As Kierkegaard states, "The very moment I talk with anyone else about that which is supreme to me, about what God's will with me is, at that very same moment God's power over me is diminished" (*JP* 2:385 #1960).[82]

Silence, then, is for Kierkegaard inseparably connected with the task of becoming religious. Accordingly, the quality of silence that Climacus attributes to Lessing appears in a specifically God-related context. After lauding the fact that Lessing, in his polemic relationship to Christianity, betrays no hint of the result of his probing to anyone else, Climacus observes:

> Verily, no father confessor to whom a secret has been intrusted, no maiden who has pledged herself and her love to silence and becomes

immortal through keeping her pledge, no man who takes every explanation of his life with him into the grave, no one, no one could carry himself more circumspectly than Lessing, while achieving the still more difficult task of keeping silent through speaking. (*CUP* 61)

In other words, Climacus holds that Lessing, in his public theological debate, effectively masks all trace of his individual insight into Christianity and his God-relationship. That Lessing's writings contain a definite element of silence on both the personal and the tactical level is irrefutable. Once again, however, there is a marked qualitative difference between the silence of the historical Lessing and that maintained by the pseudonym.

Essentially, it is the open, honest style of Lessing's prose that renders him silent. That is: through the medium of a manner of writing which seems to draw the reader into the author's very thought process, Lessing, nevertheless, says only what he chooses to say. Behind the facade of an apparently easy, spontaneous conversational style, one detects a careful and deliberate process of weighing and balancing, a cautious evaluation of what should be stated and what left unsaid.

On the personal level, this quality of silence is illustrated in Lessing's reluctance to reveal personal feelings and emotions, which leads him to control his expression of such to the point that he can confidently declare that he has never written a line to anyone which the whole world could not read (*LS* 18:72 #378). For example, he was concerned not to share his negative feelings with others, and would often postpone writing for months at a time rather than give voice to the unpleasantness, which would naturally dominate any letters written during such a period. In his opinion:

[From such letters] you see . . . how stupidly and imprudently I randomly write and speak, when my heart is full of vexation and gall. What then can I do better, than just wait out my frenzy in silence, and become a burden to no-one because of it? (*LS* 18:106 #407)[83]

This tendency to silence was not restricted to negative situations. It seemed to apply equally to any circumstance of importance to Lessing. Thus, his response to the loss of a friend such as Ewald von Kleist is a plea for silence rather than a maudlin and tasteless display of literary emotion (*LS* 17:170 #122). In the same sense, death in his immediate family seems to evoke in him a desire more for action than for words. For example, when berated for his apparent failure to respond with sufficient sorrow to the death of a brother, he replies, "Why should sorrowers communicate their grief to one another, and in this way purposely intensify it?" After thus justifying his silence, he then voices his conviction that the duty laid on him by the loss of this brother is to increase his manifestation of love for his remaining siblings, thus transferring his feelings for the dead to the living (*LS* 17:204–05 #154).[84]

Even in letters to Eva König, Lessing maintains a surprising degree of reticence concerning his feelings for her and his hopes for marriage. Climacus attributes to him the ability to remain silent through speaking—one could likewise claim that to a large degree, he possesses the power to speak by remaining silent. In a sense, his silence speaks more eloquently in this context than many words, to convey his true feeling for Eva, as, for example, in the following passage when he thanks her for her letters and hints at his desires for the future:

> Accept once again my most tender, most sincere thanks for the, to be sure mute and dead, but for me still very entertaining, best, most beloved companions in my Wolfenbüttel isolation. Oh, if only—you know what I wish!—(*LS* 18:48 #365)[85]

Perhaps the most complete expression of feeling provided by Lessing is found in the well-known letters concerning the death of his son and, shortly thereafter, his wife.[86] But these statements as well seem to gain their eloquence from their terseness and brevity. In a sense, each statement is a cipher pointing to the depth of emotion concealed behind it, as for example, the pervading despair and pessimism toward the world in this statement concerning his son:

> And I lost him so reluctantly, this son! for he had so much sense! so much sense! . . . Was it not good sense, that they had to drag him into the world with iron forceps? that he immediately suspected something?—Was it not good sense that he seized the first opportunity to get away again? (*LS* 18:259 #584)[87]

However, Lessing is quick to retract even this measured show of feeling with these self-deprecating words:

> I can hardly remember what sort of tragic letter that might have been, which I supposedly wrote to you. I feel heartily ashamed, if it betrays the slightest amount of despair. Besides, not despair, but rather imprudence is my shortcoming, which sometimes expresses itself just a bit bitterly and misanthropically. (*LS* 18:261 #587)

In conjunction with this reluctance to betray too much personal feeling, it should also be noted that Lessing would, at times, summarily break off a discussion when it appeared that it was about to leave the realm of ideas and descend to the level of a clash of individual opinions.[88]

The aforementioned conscious concealment appears, at least in part, to be the product of Lessing's conception of authorial anonymity, which presupposes the absence of personal expression in literary works. In addition to this type of reticence, a marked element of tactical silence is evident in Lessing's writing. One obvious reason for the employment of such strategic means was the political climate of Lessing's age. As Lessing's own experience in the theological debate with Goeze illustrates, the power of the censor was still undisputed, a fact that often had a direct impact on both the writing style and the choice of material selected by authors. And even beyond the everpresent threat of censorship, it was necessary for authors to protect their own position and livelihood, as well as the possibility for future publication and performance of their works, by keeping a close watch on what they chose to say and how they expressed it. As Lessing laconically observes in this connection: "a fool is willing to write everything he thinks" (*LS* 17:296 #235).[89]

This type of cautious restraint and manner of leaving unstated much that could be said, likewise appears as an integral characteristic of Lessing's polemic procedure. For example, he often chooses merely to ignore an opponent's challenge rather than to re-prove a point that he has already made elsewhere, or to discuss something that he feels to be self-evident. He also demonstrates a marked reluctance to make statements of personal conviction that are too direct, to the degree that one would almost have to apply the words of Falk to him:

> I am now so accustomed to this expression. Of course, not as if I had a lack of personal conviction: but rather because I do not prefer to directly block someone's path. (*LS* 13:344)[90]

Lack of System

Kierkegaard believed that the Hegelian predilection to objective systematization had contributed largely to the destruction of true Christianity, because it had reduced religion to a compendium of beliefs, which could be repeated *ad absurdum* without personal involvement or risk. For this reason, Lessing's failure to produce any recognizable system of results takes on particular significance in the context of the pseudonym. As Climacus asserts:

> With respect to the religious, [Lessing] always had something that he kept to himself, something which he did indeed give utterance to, but in so artful a manner that it could not be repeated after him directly and by rote; something which always remained the same while it constantly changed its form; something which was not stereotyped for insertion in a systematic formulary. . . .
>
> It was a shame of Lessing thus to place all those who are so infinitely willing to swear in *verba magistri*, in the embarrassing position of never being able, in relation to him, to assume the only attitude natural to them, namely, the attitude of taking an oath. It was a shame he did not say outright: "I attack Christianity," so that the swearers could say: "We take our oath on the same;" or that he did not say outright: "I defend Christianity," so that the swearers could say: "We take our oath on the same." (*CUP* 64)

In other words, the Lessing pseudonym appears as a dialectical gymnast who withdraws himself, along with his insight and subjectivity, at every juncture where one who wishes merely to externally possess a category of belief might find a firm handhold, thus leaving would-be believers with nothing concrete on which to support themselves.

Lessing's lack of formal or systematic results has indeed been an anathema to critics and scholars from the very first. In reality, it is precisely this lack of formal statement, or perhaps more accurately, the existence of so many apparently contradictory statements that has given rise to the interpretive confusion which continues to surround Lessing and his work.

Although characteristically the Lessing pseudonym consciously and ironically avoids direct systematic statement in order to purposely foil uncommitted "oath-swearers," a careful study of the work of the historical Lessing reveals the fact that his lack of systematic result was actually determined to a major degree by outside forces. Among the most powerful of these external determinants was the state of extreme financial want in which he existed during the entirety of his career as a writer. As he exclaims to his brother, "Even the most successful authorship is the most wretched trade" (*LS* 17:311 #251). The nature of the material Lessing produced was often the direct result of financial exigency, which required that he write that which he could complete quickly and sell for a profit. This situation finds direct expression in Lessing's statement to Karl:

> After this, however, I strongly advise you to write less, that is, to publish less and study all the more for yourself. I assure you, that on my part I would follow this advice far more myself, if my circumstances did not compel me to write so much. Since I can barely make ends meet with my regular salary, so I have absolutely no other means to work my way little by little out of my debts, than to write. God knows, I have never needed to write for money more than now: and this necessity naturally has an influence even on the material about which I write. (*LS* 17:348 #279)

Perhaps the best example of this plight is the fact that Lessing invested so much time in the *Wolfenbütteler Beiträge* (Wolfenbüttel Articles), for which he was guaranteed publication, even though he felt that such dry scholarly research served only to deaden his creative spirit.[91] It should also be noted in this connection that the nature and subject matter of relatively large portions of Lessing's production were determined directly by the official position he occupied at the time; in addition to the *Beiträge*, one need only point to the *Dramaturgy* for an illustration of this fact.

Further external determinants of the nature of Lessing's work would be the political climate of the time and the ever-present threat of censorship. For example, as Lessing's statements show, he turned to the dramatic form of *Nathan* as a vehicle for completing the theological debate with Goeze after the censor had expressly forbidden all further polemic involvement on the subject.[92]

Of even greater significance as an obstacle to the systematic presentation of thought is the polemic structural component of by far the greater portion of Lessing's writing. This type of work is not produced in response to a personal creative impulse; rather, it consists in a reply to an assertion made by someone else. This method of procedure is readily evident in the fact that the *Literaturbriefe* (Letters on Literature) and individual sections of the *Dramaturgy* respond directly to statements, actions, or techniques employed by writers such as Gottsched, Voltaire, Diderot, and Shakespeare, as well as to stage productions and actors with whom Lessing was personally involved.

Likewise, *Laokoon* takes its impetus from an assertion made by Johann Winckelmann, and the entire Reimarus Fragment debate, which ultimately culminates in *Nathan,* begins as Lessing's response to ideas expressed in the Reimarus manuscript. Lessing's advice to critical writers, in fact, is specifically that they find someone with whom they can debate—in this way they will little by little find material about which to write, and the rest will take care of itself.[93] This type of response to the assertions of the opponent automatically precludes any sort of systematic development of ideas. Rather, the ideas ripen through the course of the debate, a fact that accounts for much of the apparent inconsistency in concepts over a period of time. The point of departure is the polemic attack, not a preconceived and preordered system of thought that is to be expounded. It is particularly in this point that Lessing's enthusiasm for the hunt rather than the catch becomes most evident.[94] Since the structure of polemic debate automatically presupposes response and defense rather than aggressive assertion, it naturally occurs that the direction and themes of an extended debate are largely determined by the position of the opponent, who at times may stray far afield from the original inquiry. As Lessing complains in an ironic remark to a fictional "Mutter Else" (Mother Else):

> But just realize, Else, that I am not the assailing party, but rather the one under attack, and therefore must go along everywhere where your minister, the Chief Pastor, Mr. Goeze drags me. To be sure, he hauls me to many places, where we both have no business being: but is that my fault? (*LS* 13:203)

The polemic investigation of truth thus postulates only the debate, and leaves the conclusions open to the course that the discussion happens to follow. Clearly this form of inquiry is the very antithesis of the systematization so abhorred by Kierkegaard, because it cannot operate on the basis of a predetermined superstructure of ideas.

In addition to the points already mentioned, Lessing's failure to produce a compendium of results is also determined by his own individual style of thought and production. Because he conceives truth to be a process rather than a possession, his work retains the character of an exploration of possibilities rather than the presentation of definitive conclusions. The open culmination of the *Erziehung* (Education of the Human Race), with its hints at reincarnation, the equally open-ended "Ring Parable" in *Nathan*, and the parable of the "Burning Palace" are illustrations of this fact. For Lessing, the truth is of prime importance, not the shape of the system that presents it. As he states: "If the medicine is salutary, it does not matter how one administers it to the child" (*LS* 4:405). And again, "If the paralytic experiences the salutary shocks of the electric spark: what is it to him, whether Nollet or whether Franklin, or whether neither one of the two is right?" (*LS* 13:134).[95]

It is, in fact, inadequate merely to assert that Lessing *failed* to produce systematic results, because it was never his intention to do so, particularly because he preferred the play of possibilities in conceptual development. For example, in conjunction with his production of the *Erziehung* (Education of the Human Race), he describes himself in the third person in these terms:

> The Education of the Human Race is by a good friend, who is fond of constructing diverse hypotheses and systems, in order to have the pleasure of demolishing them again. (*LS* 18:269 #597)

After expressing the fact that the *Erziehung* radically contradicts the goals of the *Ungennanter* (the anonymous writer) in the Reimarus debate, he continues: "But what does it matter? Each should speak what appears to him to be truth, and may the truth itself be commended to God!" (Ibid.).

With great assurance, Lessing declares his philosophical and theological independence in these terms:

> I am an admirer of theology, and not a theologian. I have not been compelled to take an oath upon any certain system. Nothing obliges me to speak any language other than my own. I pity all honest men, who are not fortunate enough to be able to say this of themselves. (*LS* 13:109)

This idea of speaking his own language is not unrelated to Lessing's concept of genius, in which, after a solid foundation of study has been established, all thought and rules of presentation flow naturally from within, rather than being applied mechanically from without.

In addition to the polemic structure of Lessing's production, his style of writing itself serves effectively to hinder any sort of systematic elaboration of his thought. His is a conversational style that flows relatively naturally as a dialogue with the reader. For this reason, his thought finds its most comfortable expression in the concise form of the open letter, and most often draws on imagery such as simile and metaphor to illustrate his point. Such a medium is hardly suited to the systematic exposition of concepts, in which hypotheses must be supported by formal proofs. Lessing prefers a greater flexibility of presentation, often clothing himself in the guise of sympathy with one negative party in order to better reveal the errors of another standpoint. Emil Staiger notes that the direction of thought presented by Lessing does not arise from the guiding role of logic; rather, it appears as an association of ideas that originate in the metaphorical language which Lessing employs. Staiger continues:

> Naturally, logic remains fundamentally discernable with Lessing. But the surface appears to be as fortuitous as any dispute between two individuals of differing belief and temperament. The dialogues therefore never impress one as being constructed, but rather as being as vigorous as life itself.[96]

Section III: Lessing the Ironic Communicator

Lessing communicates in an ironic form
calculated to confuse and dismay the unwary.

Communication and Literary Style

Because of the constant tension that he perceives between religious interiority and the world of appearances, in addition to the inevitable impossibility of finding adequate expression for matters of subjective inwardness, Kierkegaard is deeply concerned with the question of communication. Existing individuals cannot sufficiently reveal through the medium of language that which they experience within the isolation of their subjectivity, since existence is reality and language is ideality. As Kierkegaard asserts:

> When I seek to express sense perception in this way [i.e., through language], the contradiction is present, for what I say is something different from what I want to say. I cannot express reality in language, because I use ideality to characterize it, which is a contradiction, an untruth. (*JP* 3:6–7 #2320)

Because of this inherent difficulty, Kierkegaard turns from a direct to an indirect form of communication, as being the more viable form for the expression of truth.[97]

The choice between the employment of a direct or an indirect method of communication is determined by the subject matter to be presented. Factual knowledge, which is occupied with "insignificant" truths, and theoretical statements that require no application in the individual life, can be communicated in a direct manner. These truths can be termed "insignificant" because they are truth regardless of whether or not they are accepted by an individual. On the other hand, "concerned truth," as presented in an ethical or religious sense, deals not so much with subject matter, as with the impetus to direct application through action in the personal existence. This is especially important within the religious sphere since, to Kierkegaard, Christianity is an attitude toward life, an actualization of belief, rather than merely a doctrine. It is this type of "concerned truth" that can only be communicated to others indirectly. There can be no teacher or learner in either ethical or religious matters, because the teacher is her/himself the learner in the sense that an individual can never fully execute the demands of religion or ethics. To quote the formulation by Lars Bejerholm, who speaks solely in terms of the ethical, though the concept applies equally to the religious:

> The way of communication must reflect the ethical subject-matter with its incessant demand to each individual, and it must reflect the absolute character of that demand, it must reflect the fact that each individual is obliged to execute the demand in his own life, regardless of how others do it. Hence, there is no pupil-dependence in ethical questions. He who delivers an ethical message must, therefore, execute it himself. . . . He must not expound ethics as a finite, consummate whole, but rather as a program for action; he must not gather devoted pupils, but rather prepare the receiver of ethical communication for independence. In brief, he must be a Socratic Maieutic.[98]

The search for and appropriation of truth is something that the individual must do for him- or herself. For this reason, the most any person can do for others is to attempt to shake them from their illusions and their confidence in the external rather than internal modes of existence.[99] The important function of irony in this process cannot be overlooked. For Kierkegaard, irony is more than merely a literary device; it is a way of experiencing the world, an incipient form of subjectivity that constitutes a transitional border stage between the aesthetic and the ethical spheres. Additionally, it is a form of communication bound to reflection, an "infinite absolute negativity."

> In its didactic function irony becomes in the hands of Kierkegaard an instrument for disabusing his readers of what is not personally appropriated, of stripping away what is not permeated with consciousness and enjoyed. It is not the truth but surely the way, albeit the negative way, whereby illusion and imaginary results forsake him.

Thus the profoundly serious aim of the ironic banter that pervades the greater part of Kierkegaard's authorship is to bring his contemporaries back to actuality and to truth.[100]

It is in respect to the concept of literary style that the Lessing figure presented by Climacus comes closest to the historical Lessing. In fact, it could be said that the essential ideality which Climacus crystallizes out of the historical figure is to a large degree the actual embodiment of the style itself. That is, the pseudonym Lessing is the spirit of Lessing's style endowed with human form. Kierkegaard's polemic against the Hegelians is also very evident in this reference, because the traits cited by Climacus are once again those which foil the attempts of any who wish to repeat by rote, since these characteristics cannot be impressed into the service of the world-historical and the systematic.

In relationship to Lessing's style, Climacus first asserts:

> Lessing was no serious man. His entire mode of communication is without earnestness, being lacking in that true dependability which suffices for others, namely, those who always think in the wake of someone else, though without thoughtfulness. (*CUP* 64)

This statement once again refers to Lessing's lack of system and his failure to offer any quotable results in his theological and philosophical writings. Climacus then continues:

> And now his style! This polemic tone, which every instant has unlimited leisure to indulge in a witticism, and that even in a period of ferment; for according to an old newspaper I have found, the age was then precisely as now in such a ferment of change that the world has never seen the like. (Ibid., 64–65)

One of the most characteristic points of Lessing's style is, indeed, the leisurely and spontaneous conversational form of presentation, particularly in the polemic works. This style serves to draw the reader in an affable, charming manner into a sense of intimate "in-the-know" dialogue with the writer. Lessing's portrayal of himself as a *Spaziergänger* (stroller)[101] very aptly describes the unhurried character of his published exposition, in contrast to the formal purposiveness of most traditional philosophical presentations. The readers seem, indeed, to be privy to the author's very thought process. As Wilhelm Mummenhoff observes:

> If with many authors we must first overcome the presentation, in order to

be able to penetrate through it to the thought, which it envelops like fog; in comparison, with Lessing the presentation is so vivid and clear, and the thought springs forth at first sight so vigorously, purely and serenely, that it almost seems as if it has penetrated directly from the intellect of the thinker into our own, without clothing itself first in external raiment.[102]

This fact becomes clear when, for example, Lessing in *Laokoon* openly declares his intention to write down his thoughts in the order in which they occur to him.[103] Likewise, the reader is characteristically party to Lessing's debate with himself as to the material that he should present in the final number of the *Dramaturgy* (*LS* 10:208 ff.).[104] This effect of privileged presence in the author's mind is further heightened by the numerous apostrophes and exclamations, which convey the impression that one is overhearing the author in a running dialogue with himself. "But I am lingering over trifles" (*LS* 9:111) he exclaims in *Laokoon*, and again, "But I am wandering off course" (*LS* 9:14). In the midst of a polemic attack on Goeze he breaks off, exclaiming "But I am forgetting myself" (*LS* 13:102). In the *Literaturbriefe* (Letters on Literature) he admits "But I think I am starting to deride; and I do not really wish to do that" (*LS* 8:28). We see him breaking off an argument with a sudden "Doch halt!" (But wait!) and then starting off in another direction (*LS* 13:196); we hear him ask himself "Heigh-ho! Where did I wish to go with the previous [argument]?" (*LS* 13:187) and again "But to what purpose all of this prattle?" (*LS* 13:151).

Emil Staiger observes that Lessing chooses this form of presentation because he desires to arouse in the reader a sense of the same delight in the process of thought as he himself feels. This result is only possible, however, when the actual *source* of the thought is presented, rather than merely its final formulation.[105]

One element of this apparent immediate authorial accessibility—which incidentally serves as a devastating weapon against the defensiveness of Lessing's opponents—is the intimate, ingratiating sense of honesty that he conveys in both his public and his private writings. One finds no trace of distress in his admission: "To all these questions, I know nothing to answer; in spite of the fact that for a long time I have made it my business to be able to answer them" (*LS* 12:160). Or again, in reference to some particularly enigmatic poems: "I say: one should judge for himself. I for my part do not trust myself to judge. Because, unfortunately, I do not understand them" (*LS* 12:107).[106] This type of openness proves to be impenetrable to the attacker, who cannot accuse Lessing, because he has already accused himself.

The fact that Lessing's writing style does indeed indulge in witticism hardly needs to be proven. His often bitingly ironic observations occur in a broad spectrum of intensity. At the one end, one finds tongue-in-cheek barbs aimed at friends such as Gleim, who has failed to send Lessing a promised copy of his latest work:

> Make sure that I receive it, or—Or I will criticize your translation of Anacreon most cruelly. You think perhaps to elude this threat, if you do not send it to me. Oh, I can criticize it without having read it. (*LS* 17:154 #106)

Into this category also falls the laconic statement concerning C. A. Klotz: "I was afraid that Klotz would also wish to butt into the game: but this time the man has proven himself to be more astute than I would have thought,—he died" (*LS* 18:5 #336).[107]
At the other end of the spectrum is the bitter polemic invective that Lessing employs to humiliate and publicly annhilate his opponents. Among the prime examples of this type of wit is the long one-sided dialogue that Lessing holds with Goeze who, Lessing alleges, is talking in his sleep (*LS* 13:56 ff.). In addition, Lessing reduces Goeze to invisibility in the 8th *Anti-Goeze*, by eliminating him from the conversation and, in his presence, discussing him with "noble Houyhnhnm," the post horse (*LS* 13:187 ff.).[108]
Climacus continues his description of Lessing's style by citing:

> This stylist equanimity, which develops a simile in minutest detail, as if the literary expression had a value in itself, as if peace and safety reigned; and that although perhaps the printer's devil and world-history and all mankind stood waiting for him to have it finished. (*CUP* 65)

Once again, the predilection of Lessing's writing to the frequent use of poetic imagery such as the simile, metaphor, allegory, and parable needs no argument. Because this metaphoric usage forms the basis of one of the prime complaints that Goeze lodges against Lessing, it is possible to gain insight into Lessing's own understanding of his techniques through a consideration of his defense. At the outset, Lessing refers to his style almost as if it were something outside himself, over which he has no control:

> Every individual has his own style, just as his own nose; and it is neither polite nor Christian to make fun of an honest man because of his nose, no matter how peculiar it is. Is it my fault that I do not have a different style? That I am not affecting it, I am aware. I am also aware that

it tends to make the most novel cascades when I have most fully pondered the issue. It often plays with the material all the more mischievously, the more I have previously attempted to gain command of it through cold reflection. (*LS* 13:149)

He then insists that the important thing is not how one writes, but rather, how one thinks, and throws Goeze's assertion that metaphoric words conceal unclear thought back at the pastor, with the question:

And you certainly do not wish to contend . . . that no-one can think correctly and precisely, but he who avails himself of the most proper, most common, most insipid expression? that to attempt in some way to give cold, symbolic ideas something of the warmth and the life of natural symbols should by any means be injurious to the truth? (Ibid.)

Thus, in marked contrast to all those who desire to develop "cold, symbolic ideas" in the traditional form, Lessing consciously attempts to add the warmth and life of figurative speech to his presentation of the truth. Admitting that the theater may have spoiled his style to some degree, he describes his main error, which he terms as his *Erbsünde* (original sin):

Namely: it [Lessing's style] lingers over its metaphors, spins them often into parables, and occasionally amplifies them only too readily into an allegory. (Ibid., 150)

Lessing then explains how this type of style has arisen from the concern to write dramatic dialogue. As he asserts, in actual life, conversation is guided more by imagination than by reason, and, therefore, imagery must be used if one is to lend truth and pliability to the interchange. In differentiating between prose and dialogue, Lessing observes that in the former the direction of thought always remains the same, whereas in the latter it changes constantly. He then asserts:

Those [prose works] require a sedate, consistently uniform pace; this [dialogue] now and then demands leaps: and seldom is a high jumper a good, even dancer. (Ibid.)

Lessing's final assertion is that, in spite of the fact that his style demands leaps, his logic is sound: "good logic is always the same thing, be it applied to whatever one wishes" (Ibid., 151).

In response to Goeze's charge that he attempts to seize the readers' imagination through the usage of all types of unexpected imagery rather than by trying to convince them with proofs, Lessing further explains:

> I hold it not only to be advantageous, but also necessary to clothe arguments in pictures; and to characterize all the accessory notions, which one or the other awakens, through allusions. He who knows and understands nothing of this, would absolutely not wish to become an author; because all good authors became such only in this way. (*LS* 13:188–89)

From Lessing's arguments, then, it becomes clear that he develops his metaphorical presentation because he feels it does have a value in itself—that is, it gives animation, warmth, and the truth of actual life to ideas which, otherwise, would be cold, symbolic, and, therefore, far more difficult for the reader to grasp. Mummenhoff observes in this respect:

> The characteristic part of Lessing's use of imagery consists of this, as it were, vaulting amplification of a simple image into a complete painting. In a smoothly progressing presentation, one would scarcely be able to tolerate it, but in Lessing's writings, which are direct outpourings of thought and emotion, precisely those passages in which he speaks in pictures, belong among the most superb and most effective.[109]

Climacus also cites Lessing's "systematic slackness, which refuses to obey the paragraphic norm." In doing so, he is actually speaking on two levels. First, he is referring once again to the fact that Lessing not only refuses to employ a formal style of philosophical proof and argumentation, but also that he produces no systematic or methodical results.

Secondly, Climacus is alluding to a highly individual aspect of the actual mechanics of Lessing's writing style. That is, just as Lessing's usual form of exposition is modeled after the free-flowing nature of conversation, so the grammatical architecture mirrors the inflection and intonation of spoken language rather than the prescribed structure of formal prose. A liberal sprinkling of dashes, colons and exclamation points stands out on practically any page of his production. And, just as he unhesitatingly begins paragraphs with a "Doch!" (certainly) or a "Heyda!" (Heigh-ho!), so he never shies away from breaking a sentence off before it is completed, leaving the reader with only a dash and an obvious hint at how the thought should be completed. The following apostrophe to Martin Luther from the "Parabel" (Parable) provides an excellent example of these characteristics:

> O daß Er es könnte, Er, den ich am liebsten zu meinem Richter haben
> möchte! —Luther, du! —Grosser, verkannter Mann! Und von nieman-
> den mehr verkannt, als von den kurzsichtigen Starrköpfen, die, deine
> Pantoffeln in der Hand, den von dir gebahnten Weg, schreiend aber
> gleichgültig daher schlendern! —Du hast uns von dem Joche der Tradi-
> tion erlöst: wer erlöst uns von dem unerträglichern Joche des Buch-
> stabens! Wer bringt uns endlich ein Christentum, wie du es jetzt lehren
> würdest; wie es Christus selbst lehren würde! Wer– –. (*LS* 13:102)[110]

> Oh, that He could, He, whom I would most prefer to have as my judge!
> —Luther, you! —Great, misunderstood man! And by no-one more mis-
> understood than the short-sighted, bull-headed people who, your slip-
> pers in their hand, saunter screeching but apathetically along the path
> which you blazed! —You delivered us from the yoke of tradition: who
> will free us from the more insufferable yoke of the letter [of the law]!
> Who will at last bring us a Christianity such as you would now teach;
> such as Christ himself would teach! Who– –.

In place of the formal statements customarily employed in theological and philosophical elaboration, Lessing frequently uses rapid,
short questions to drive home his point and to provoke the reader to
thought. This technique is clearly visible, for example, in the following passage, which is directed against Goeze:

> Sie, Herr Pastor, Sie hätten den allergeringsten Funken Lutherischen
> Geistes? —Sie? der Sie auch nicht einmal Luthers Schulsystem zu
> übersehen im Stande sind? —. . . der Sie diesen ehrlichen Mann mit
> Steinen verfolgen?
>
> Und warum? —Weil dieser ehrliche Mann zugleich den schriftlich
> gegebenen Rat eines ungennanten Baumeisters, das Gebäude lieber ganz
> abzutragen, —gebilligt? unterstützt? ausführen wollen? auszuführen
> angefangen? —Nicht doch! —nur nicht unterschlagen zu dürfen
> geglaubt. (*LS* 13:101)[111]

> You, Pastor, you supposedly have the most negligible spark of
> Luther's spirit? —You? who are not even able to keep track of Luther's
> school system? — . . . who pursue this honest man [Lessing] with
> stones?
>
> And why? —Because the written advice of an anonymous architect,
> preferably to level the building [Christianity] entirely, was, by this hon-
> est man, —sanctioned? endorsed? Did he desire to execute it? begin to
> execute it? —Certainly not! —he only believed that he did not have the
> right to suppress it.

After remarking that through this technique of questioning the author often expresses his true meaning, Emil Staiger comments:

> Lessing questions himself while he questions the reader. The question is, to be sure, placed in such a way that the answer appears to be inevitable, that the hearer can only answer with "yes." They are, as they say, rhetorical questions. But that does not diminish their tension. To the contrary, in them is expressed the way in which an intellectual act is actually executed: we ask; a correctly placed question generates the answer of its own accord. The question is the way to understanding.[112]

It is precisely because Lessing does depart from the paragraphic norm—that is, from the steady and often ponderous development of formal prose—that his argumentation presents such a dynamic and powerfully devastating form. In this regard, Walter Jens observes:

> Lessing writes for people who clap and hiss, and not for colleagues, not—or at least only secondarily—for theologians, antiquarians and artists. The interjections and questions in his letters, the flaring up and lashing out— . . . this "crushing eloquence," as Friedrich Schlegel called it, a pinning down of the opponent, an insistence and hammering, borne by anaphora that follow one another in rapid succession— . . . these fireworks require contradiction, objections and applause. It is spectator-prose, which is always accentuated with dashes and colons there, where responses are to be expected from the person under attack or from the spectators.[113]

Climacus continues his description of Lessing's style by remarking on:

> [Lessing's] mingling of jest and earnest, which makes it impossible for a third party to know which is which—unless, indeed the third party knows it by himself. This artfulness, which perhaps even sometimes puts a false emphasis upon the indifferent, so that the initiated may precisely in this manner best grasp the dialectically decisive point, while the heretics get nothing to run with. (*CUP* 65)

In a very real sense, Lessing's manner of writing often unabashedly clothes even the most serious of observations in elements of wit and irony, a combination that serves not only to mask his own point of view, but also to unmask the follies he detects in the standpoint presented by others. A classic example of this practice can be found in Lessing's statement concerning Klopstock's defense of religion: "He knows how to awaken in his readers the wish that Christianity would be true; supposing, of course, that we should be so unfortunate that it were not true" (*LS* 4:405). This ironic tone is not above a playful (and therefore dangerously wounding) praise of the opponent, as when Lessing expresses sympathy with Goeze in these terms:

> God forbid that my readers should believe that I myself would be able to say such a thing about my neighbor! I do not know why I should feel indignation towards a man for whom I have pity. And one must well have pity for a man who can hold the reasoning which follows to be so conclusive, that he may accompany it with a trump-card. (*LS* 13:68–69)

In the same manner, Lessing is ironically willing to excuse his opponents, and thereby implicitly condemn them all the more:

> That is not the correct conception of my thoughts, venerable man. However, it cannot really have been your intention to make such a false presentation of my thoughts. You were too hasty, out of confidence in your good cause, which you indeed supposed to have been attacked by me: you acted precipitately. (*LS* 13:99)[114]

As a vehicle against which to display the jesting seriousness of his polemic, Lessing presents the opponent, or the "other," as a figure, a marionette with which he holds a one-sided dialogue. Unlike Kierkegaard's pseudonyms, who in a sense have life in themselves, and who represent an independent world view, Lessing's figures are more like cardboard puppets against which he can aim his polemic darts, or in a more positive sense, mirrors against which he directs the piercing ray of his argument. In this sense, the Goeze of the *Fragmentenstreit* (Fragment Controversy) is not the living, breathing historical pastor, any more than the post horse Houyhnhnm is an actual animal. Both are shadows, dramatic creations against which the ironic earnestness of Lessing's polemic search for truth becomes visible.[115]

That Lessing did, indeed, mingle jest and earnestness in his writing is indisputable. That this practice at times caused confusion is equally clear, as is evidenced, for example, by the discussion with Jacobi concerning Spinozism. Particularly for strategic reasons, Lessing at times conveyed the appearance of defending a viewpoint other than his own. As he explains: "I get along with my open enemies, so that I can better be on guard against the concealed ones" (*LS* 18:227 #546).[116]

The final statement made by Climacus concerning Lessing's style reads as follows:

This form of his, so completely an expression of his individuality, spontaneously and refreshingly cutting its own path, not dying away in a mosaic of catchwords and authorized phrases and contemporary slogans, which in quotation marks give evidence that the writer keeps up with the times, while Lessing on the other hand confides to the reader *sub rosa* that he keeps up with the thought. (*CUP* 65)

Once again, Climacus speaks on two levels. On the surface, he emphasizes Lessing's individuality of expression, which enables him to remain at the forefront of intellectual progression without binding him to language foreign to him. At a deeper level, however, Kierkegaard once again aims a barb at the Hegelians, who, in his opinion, were bogged down precisely in a mosaic of catchwords, phrases, and slogans derived from the System, which they adopted in order to keep up with the times, rather than in response to any particular individual conviction.

The foregoing analysis has established the main points of the historical Lessing's factual existence in relationship to Climacus' description of the Lessing pseudonym. We now turn to an analysis of the data that have been presented in this section. Accordingly, Section III addresses the following topics: (1) the viability of Kierkegaard's attempt to abstract a historical figure into the world of the pseudonyms; (2) the actual significance of Lessing's pseudonymity in the overall complex of the pseudonyms; (3) the nature and significance of the differences between the historical and the pseudonymic Lessing; and (4) the reasons why, out of all possible historical personalities, Lessing was chosen to be transported into the sphere of the pseudonyms.

3

The Significance of Lessing's Pseudonymity in the Overall Complex of the Pseudonyms

Abstracting a Historical Figure into a Pseudonym

As has been established previously, the Lessing of the *Postscript*, like every figure or being employed in the service of indirect communication, is in actuality a pseudonym. In bringing the Lessing pseudonym to concretion, Kierkegaard/Climacus has attempted to penetrate the historical Lessing's masks and poses, to shake off the weight of historical factuality, and to reveal the lightness of pure ideality that he perceives in Lessing's essence. This attempt to import the inner essentiality of a historical figure into a literary or philosophical realm is certainly not a new one, although, as is the case with practically any influence, philosophical, literary or other, which impinged on his sphere of productivity, Kierkegaard transformed older custom into something uniquely his own. In this context, a very relevant discussion of the relationship of historical figures to literary production can, in fact, be found in Lessing's own writings.

In the *Hamburg Dramaturgy*, Lessing attempts to establish with some precision the exact role of the author, in this case, dramatist, as he/she chooses characters from history and attempts to endow them with dramatic form. Responding to critics who have condemned a certain play because it did not adhere closely enough to historical fact, Lessing turns first to Aristotle's statement in the *Poetics*:

> it is not the function of the poet to relate what has happened, but what may happen,—what is possible according to the law of probability or

78

necessity. The poet and the historian differ not by writing in verse or in prose. . . .The true difference is that one relates what has happened, the other what may happen. Poetry, therefore, is a more philosophical and a higher thing than history: for poetry tends to express the universal, history the particular.[1]

Lessing develops and deepens this statement in the *Hamburg Dramaturgy*, in that he asserts that tragedy is far more than history in dialogue. In fact, for the theater, history is merely a repository of names, to which we by custom attach certain character traits (*HD* 63). As he states:

> For the dramatic poet is no historian, he does not relate to us what was once believed to have happened, but he really produces it again before our eyes, and produces it again not on account of mere historical truth but for a totally different and a nobler aim. Historical accuracy is not his aim, but only the means by which he hopes to attain his aim; he wishes to delude us and touch our hearts through this delusion. (*HD* 32)

And further:

> Now Aristotle has long ago decided how far the tragic poet need regard historical accuracy: not farther than it resembles a well-constructed fable wherewith he can combine his intentions. He does not make use of an event because it really happened, but because it happened in such a manner as he will scarcely be able to invent more fitly for his present purpose. If he finds this fitness in a true case, then the true case is welcome; but to search through history books does not reward his labour. (*HD* 51)

For this reason, Lessing insists, it would be absurd to follow authors with a chronology in hand, to try them before the judgement seat of history, to demand that they back up every date, every situation with absolute historical proof. To do this would be to misrepresent the purposes of drama entirely (*HD* 62). That which is important to the dramatist is the *inner* truth of the character:

> It is assumed quite without reason, that it is one of the objects of the stage, to keep alive the memory of great men. For that we have history and not the stage. From the stage we are not to learn what such and such an individual man has done, but what every man of a certain character would do under certain given circumstances. The object of tragedy is more philosophical than the object of history, and it is de-

grading her from her true dignity to employ her as a mere panegyric of famous men or to misuse her to feed national pride. (*HD* 51–52)

As he affirms in another piece:

I know full well that the sentiments in a drama must be in accordance with the assumed character of the person who utters them. They can therefore not bear the stamp of absolute truth, it is enough if they are poetically true, if we must admit that this character under these circumstances, with these passions could not have judged otherwise. But on the other hand this poetical truth must also approach to the absolute. (*HD* 11)

Lessing asks rhetorically why it is that a poet chooses to use actual names. "Does he take his characters out of these names, or does he take these names because the characters that history lends to them have more or less resemblance to the characters that he intends to portray in his plot?" (*HD* 61). And further, "is it the mere facts, the circumstances of time and place, or is it the characters of the persons that make the facts a reality, that have induced the author to choose this fact rather than another as the subject of his play?" (*HD* 61–62). He then answers his own questions in this way:

If it is the characters, then the question is instantly decided how far the poet may depart from historical accuracy. In all that does not concern the characters, as far as he likes. Only the characters must remain sacred to him. To strengthen these, to depict them in their best light is all that he may add on his own account: the smallest essential change would annul the reasons why they bear these and not other names, and nothing offends us more than that for which we can find no reason. (*HD* 62)

At another point he concludes:

We regard the facts as something accidental, as something that may be common to many persons; the characters we regard as something individual and intrinsic. The poet may take any liberties he likes with the former so long as he does not put the facts into contradiction with the characters; the characters he may place in full light but he may not change them, the smallest change seems to destroy their individuality and to substitute in their place other persons, false persons, who have usurped strange names and pretend to be what they are not. (*HD* 96–97)

By choosing a particular name, one is actually choosing the universal qualities linked with that name, rather than particularly individual traits. For example, as Lessing points out, Aristophanes chose the name "Socrates," not because he desired to immortalize the unique individual Athenian, but rather because he wished to make all the Sophists who were involved with educating young men look foolish. Aristophanes was dealing with the dangers of the Sophists in general, and he picked the name Socrates, because Socrates had been condemned by the people as such a Sophist. For this reason, one finds traits in the Socrates presented by Aristophanes, that do not actually fit the historical Socrates. But Lessing finishes:

> how much is the nature of the comedy misapprehended, if these inexact traits be regarded as nothing but arbitrary calumnies, and not regarded as that which they are, enlargement of the individual characters, an elevation from the personal to the general. (*HD* 236)

In summary, then, according to Lessing, the actual incidents and anecdotes surrounding the daily life of the historical person have little relevance to that which an author wishes to accomplish. The dramatist is free to invent any number of circumstances or events. That which is of utmost importance is that the character itself remain essentially true to the traits automatically and traditionally associated with the particular name which has been chosen. A Bonaparte without ambition or a gentle, loving Medusa would, according to Lessing's view, be a gross falsification, a usurpation of a familiar name by a foreign character. However, it is not enough that the figure presented merely retain the essential internal qualities generally associated with the particular name. Lessing also insists that a character or figure is *only* of value in a literary text if it applies more broadly to universal humanity—that is, if it draws the readers/viewers into a wider context and greater universal understanding than they could attain through mere factual contact with a historical figure.[2]

That Kierkegaard is in basic agreement with Lessing's assessment of the relationship of the historical to the poetic/dramatic becomes quite clear through his own treatment of historical figures, as well as through the statements he makes in the authorship. Apart from the theological question of whether faith can be based on historical fact, Kierkegaard's relationship to history as such is generally one of mistrust, tending toward animosity.

A part of this aversion to historical fact stems, of course, from Kierkegaard's ongoing battle against the Hegelian system. As Kierkegaard argues:

> We humans flatter ourselves that world history is enormously important, something which therefore must also attract considerable attention from God.
>
> Is not this faith in the immense importance of history one of the human delusions which aim to sustain and enliven a zest for life, the desire to join the hubbub stirred up by the stories of the devilish uproar and hullabaloo all these various emperors and kings made while they lived?
>
> nowadays . . . everything is preserved for history, the enormous mass of insignificant material is dragged in . . . so that the concept of history is completely abolished. (*JP* 4:598–99 #5035)

In his opinion, then, a mass of historical information can prove nothing, and is, in fact, only an unnecessary obstruction to the subjectivity of the existing individual.

The second quarrel that Kierkegaard has with history concerns those who are busily involved in systematizing the accidental occurences of an individual life, as if these contingent externals could be the proof of what was significant in that person. As he complains, "when I am dead, how busy all the assistant professors will be stripping me and mine, what competition to say the same thing, if possible, in more beautiful language—as if that were what matters" (*JP* 6:522 #6897). In his view, then, the frenzied fixation on historical fact is sheer gossipy busy-work, which deflects one's attention away from that which is truly essential. Such avid interest in minute personal details is akin to Climacus' argument against the seeming advantage of contemporaneity. As Robert C. Roberts points out, any edge gained by the contemporary of Christ is purely aesthetic, relating to the eyes, ears, nostrils, or to sheer curiosity. Thus, this apparently superior vantage point is merely of relative value, because such historical trifles have no importance in terms of essence and truth.[3] Similarly, in Kierkegaard's view, all "assistant professors" or others who collect a store of details about himself, about Lessing, or any other historical figure in the authorship, have assembled purely aesthetic data whose worth, in relationship to the authorship, are purely illusory, an attempt to tap internal spiritual richness, as it were, through external, concrete means, as if one were to attempt to touch God by using a steam shovel. The wrong tool, the wrong category is being employed, and so success is doomed from the outset.

Thus, it is clear that, within Kierkegaard's basic philosophical outlook, there is a definite difference between the historical moment, which is the point of decision for an individual, and the facts of history as such. In an attempt to clarify this conceptual dichotomy, Mark Taylor has made a useful distinction between "spatialized time" and "life-time" in Kierkegaard's thought. According to Taylor's definition, "spatialized time is based on an examination of objects, while life-time is based on a study of subjects or selves." In this sense, the facts of history fall under the heading of spatialized time, in which persons are treated much like objects, and the primary concern becomes chronology, rather than human purposes or the importance of the events.[4] It is this spatialized time, then, which has so little significance for Kierkegaard, a point that has great impact on his assimilation of historical figures into the pseudonymic sphere.

In the *Fragments*, Climacus asserts:

> The past is not necessary, since it came into existence; it did not become necessary by coming into existence . . .; still less does it become necessary through someone's apprehension of it. (*PF* 98)

His conclusion, though it applies specifically to the relationship between historical fact and faith, by implication also refers to the relationship between fact and the poetic ideal: "coming into existence has an elusiveness by which even the most dependable fact is rendered doubtful" (*PF* 100). Just as faith cannot have as its foundation the nonnecessary elusiveness of historical fact, so the ideality that is intended to challenge and provoke the individual into serious contemplation and choice must avoid the quicksand of the historical. History can only have value in a poetized form. Kierkegaard defines this process as follows: "What does it mean to poetize? It means to contribute ideality. The poet takes an actuality which lacks something of ideality and adds to it, and this is the poem" (*JP* 4:222 #4301). He states the goal of this poeticization further in this way: "That the mass is to be confronted by the ideal through the aid of a 'poet' . . . means that everyone is to be a single individual and that as a single individual he relates himself to the ideal." He then concludes, "when he says: I am a poet, only a poet—he is saying: Look at me and see that I am not great, I am not the ideal—but look at the ideal" (*JP* 4:177–78 #4198). Of himself, Kierkegaard directly states:

> I received permission to use the ideals *poetically*. . . . I am a poet—alas only a poet. But I can present Christianity in the glory of its ideality; and that I have done. . . . Do not look at my life—and yet, do look at my life only to see what a mediocre Christian I am, something you will see

> best when you listen to what I say about the ideal. Listen to that and
> never mind about my trifling person. (*JP* 6:377–78 #6727)

This agrees with Kierkegaard's statement in the *Postscript* that the
person is a fool who drags around the weight of his (Kierkegaard's)
own personal reality instead of the ideality of the poetically actual
author (*CUP* 553). For the reader of the *Postscript*, in confrontation
with the poetically ideal presentation of the subjectively existing individual, it would be as foolish to tow along the burden of Lessing's
personal existence as it would be to haul in historical facts about
Kierkegaard—such phenomena simply have no place or relevance in
the authorship.

It is the inner essentiality of the character that is of importance to
Kierkegaard—in Lessing's terms, "he wishes to delude us and touch
our hearts through this delusion" (*HD* 32) by "strengthening the
character and depicting it in its best light" (*HD* 62). What we see in
Kierkegaard is his own peculiar way of "enlarging the individual
characters and elevating them from the personal to the general" (*HD*
236). Although in the work of many authors, the transition from a
finite historical individual to an ideal universal figure seems to be
quite a straightforward process, in Kierkegaard this is more problematic. Georg Lukács, in describing the "gesture" of Kierkegaard's
life, has observed: "The gesture is the leap by which the soul . . .
leaves the always relative facts of reality to reach the eternal certainty of forms."[5] Indeed, perhaps the best description of the
process by which a historical personage becomes a Kierkegaardian
figure would be in terms of such a leap. The challenge in the attempt
to abstract a historical figure into a poetized or idealized form, in
Lessing's view, is to present the character in its best light and elevate
it to a higher universal context, although at the same time retaining
its essential internal integrity as a specific person. For the purposes
of this analysis, it would, perhaps, be most relevant to ask whether it
is actually possible for Kierkegaard to accomplish the leap and absorb a figure such as Lessing into his thought-sphere and yet leave
its character intrinsically intact. There are, indeed, three major pitfalls that jeopardize Kierkegaard's enterprise from the outset.

The first of these challenges lies in the fact that the historical
Lessing purposely masked his own personal opinions and convictions, as well as the reasons for many of his beliefs and actions. In
reality, in the history of German literature, few authors have been
subject to such voluminous and generally contradictory discussion
as Lessing. Beginning at his death in 1781, researchers have produced a literal flood of critical literature concerning his life, his

works, his character, and his influence on German society and culture, and yet this research has yielded very few final answers. Reception by readers and critics alike has constantly been plagued by innumerable questions, most of which still remain unsettled: Was Lessing a systematic or a nonsystematic thinker? Can he be regarded as a true philosopher? Was he a poet or were his works mechanical products of ratiocination? Did he follow Leibniz or Spinoza, was he an atheist or a true disciple of Luther? Was he revolutionary or reactionary, rational or irrational? Was he the prophet of progressive humanity, the embodiment of the "German Spirit," a crusader for the rights of the middle-class?

There is no question that both Lessing's writings and his personal actions often appeared to be ambiguous, even to his associates. The ideas that he conveyed, and his motives for presenting them, were very often misunderstood by his readers, largely because of the style in which he delivered them. Lewis Beck might have been speaking with many of Lessing's contemporaries when he, in a rather negative estimation of the author's stylistic characteristics, reports that Lessing's aesthetic writings are clear and straightforward, his theological writings are clear but devious, and his metaphysical works are obscure and tantalizingly brief:

> Irony was his chief weapon, but one hesitates to call him a master of irony because he seems sometimes to have been mastered by it. His flaw was that he was often too clever, with the result that almost no one knew where he stood. . . . For his irony sometimes masqueraded as ambivalence, and he disappointed his allies as often as he outraged his enemies. . . . Lessing, even while seeming to be very positive, might be merely playing with ideas and leading his interlocutor into a trap. Lessing's strategic perfidy included outright deception . . . his delight in scorning an opponent often kept him from dealing fairly with his ideas.[6]

Hans Urs von Balthasar presents a more positive view of the intriguing thinker:

> the characteristics which [Lessing] holds out to us are—riddles and masks. They shift from Christian to Enlightener, to Stoic, Spinozist and mystic, they appear to smile at that which they represent, and through their smile they appear to point even more earnestly at something which cannot be disclosed [Unenthüllbares]. That is the new, the provocative in Lessing, that he, among none but unveiled, enlightened faces, wears a mask.[7]

Lessing did indeed frequently cloak his true standpoint as part of his polemic method of argument, and also to disappear behind his literary and philosophical works, believing as he did that they, and not he, as the author, were of the utmost significance. Because these disguises have confused and confounded readers and critics for over two centuries, one might well ask how Kierkegaard can be certain that the essence, the face he discerns as he peers behind the mask, will be any more characteristic of the "true" Lessing, than that descried by anyone else in the intervening years. Or, if he is, in fact, not interested in the "true" Lessing, but rather merely in a "useful" Lessing, then does he not run an even greater risk of falsifying the character of the Lessing figure, in the way against which Lessing himself warned in the *Hamburg Dramaturgy*? In this context, Gordon Michalson's observation concerning Kierkegaard's interpretation of Lessing's ideas applies equally to the Lessing figure:

> in Kierkegaard's commentary on Lessing we are faced with the complicated case of one devil's advocate playing off of the words of another, making highly dubious the procedure of citing the interpretation of the one by the other as grounds for claiming what the views of the one being interpreted actually are.[8]

A second difficulty arises in the fact that the power of Kierkegaard's creative imagination precluded simple, uncolored contact with any idea or personality. From a number of journal entries, it can be concluded that, in a sense, Kierkegaard's prodigious creative imagination made it impossible for him to relate to any idea or personality without, at the same time, assimilating and expanding it in his own way. He often comments on the inability of a mind such as his to read and understand a book, because the great wealth of ideas triggered by the reading obstructs the meaning of the words as they were originally intended by the author. In fact, Kierkegaard found that he was unable even to write a factual account of his own life without it being colored by the inherent creativity of his mind.[9] In this regard, Niels Cappelørn warns:

> Kierkegaard had a rather pronounced tendency to treat his experiences and observations in a literary or poetic manner. Indeed, his handling of the historical is quite often shaped by his urge to poeticize. He was always more concerned with the intellectual dimension and significance of a particular situation than with its purely objective historical details. Thus he often provided rather free accounts of episodes he was describing.[10]

If Kierkegaard found himself unable even to write an account of his own life without fictionalizing it, or to read a book without absorbing and transforming the material he found, one might well wonder how there would be any possibility that he could abstract Lessing's essential universality from the historically determined and yet keep it free from Kierkegaardian shadings.

The third major danger involved in Kierkegaard's distillation of the Lessing figure is the fact that the Danish philosopher was driven by an extremely focused and powerful agenda: the desire to provoke his readers to question, to reflect, and to make decisions concerning their relationship to Christianity. Throughout his vast production, and particularly in the period following the *Postscript*, Kierkegaard insisted amply that he was and consistently had been solely a religious writer, whose entire concern had centered from the first on the question of how one can become a Christian in Christendom.[11] Driven by internal religious uncertainty, he held his prodigious ability as an author in determined focus on the Christian question. For this reason, he came to perceive himself as "a spy in a higher service, the service of the idea . . . a spy who in his spying, in learning to know all about questionable conduct and illusions and suspicious characters, all the while he is making inspection is himself under the closest inspection" (*PV* 87). This calling as a "spy" was, as he felt, an integral part of his God-relationship, because "Governance, being merciful love, employs such a person just for love's sake, saves him and educates him all the while he is employing his shrewdness, which is thus sanctified and consecrated" (*PV* 88). For this reason, in the end, he could declare of himself:

> I am he who himself has been educated, or whose authorship expresses what it is to be educated to the point of becoming a Christian. In the fact that education is pressed upon me, and in the measure that it is pressed, I press in turn upon this age; but I am not a teacher, only a fellow student. (*PV* 75)[12]

Because Kierkegaard has so clearly declared his intentions in his work, one must ask whether it is at all possible that Lessing's essence can be brought into the pseudonymic realm without being skewed from the outset.

In summary, then, because of Lessing's own unique personality and character, and because of the powerful forces of creative assimilation and absolute purpose operative in Kierkegaard's authorship, there would appear to be very little possibility that the Lessing figure, once stripped of its concrete delineating historical framework, can entirely maintain its inner truth and identity as Lessing within the sphere of the pseudonyms. It is precisely this tension between Lessing as a historical figure and the assimilative properties of Kierkegaard's mind that makes the Lessing figure so singularly important among the pseudonyms.

The Significance of Lessing's Pseudonymity

Lessing stands out within the assemblage of pseudonyms that people Kierkegaard's work, because he is entirely unique. His is the only pseudonymic figure that is derived from a historical individual whose life and work is extensively documented and documentable. For this reason, the Lessing pseudonym sheds important light on just what the "essence" that characterizes the pseudonyms *is*, and how it is derived. Because most of the pseudonyms are purely fictional, they do not offer this advantage. Even though their world view is, in all likelihood, based on the attitudes and actions of various individuals whom Kierkegaard found surrounding him in the world, it is still not possible to trace a source of origin for them.

Even the named figures in the authorship are generally less helpful in identifying this pseudonymic essence. For example, a number of scholars have devoted a great deal of effort to the analysis of Socrates, as he appears under Kierkegaard's hand.[13] It is possible to list the traits of "Kierkegaard's Socrates," as Harold Sarf does in his thorough exposition, but, in spite of one's suspicion that Kierkegaard's Socrates differs from more traditional or "historical" presentations, actual information concerning Socrates is scanty enough that it is difficult to establish exactly *what* this difference is.

The figure of Abraham is similar, in the sense that the actual information concerning him consists of relatively brief scriptural accounts. However, two studies in recent years have examined Kierkegaard's Abraham against the backdrop of Jewish tradition,[14] showing radical differences between the Jewish and the Kierkegaardian views of the Biblical patriarch. In this connection, R. Z. Friedman comes a step closer to identifying the way in which pseudonymic ideality differs from historical actuality. In a rigorous examination of Kierkegaard's Abraham in relationship to various other figures, including Socrates, as well as in a broader scriptural context than that used by Kierkegaard, Friedman concludes that "Abraham seems to be a more intense version of Socrates, but Socrates appears to be the real model for the Knight of Faith."[15]

Later he notes again, "This figure . . . is not Abraham, at least not the Abraham of the Genesis story. It is more like the Socrates of the *Apology*."[16] His conclusion: "Kierkegaard's Abraham is man on the edge; he is the Knight of Anxiety. . . . Rather than challenging us through the presentation of Abraham, Kierkegaard gives us the anxious selves we know ourselves to be. He has found us in Scripture, but lost Abraham."[17]

George Pattison has demonstrated quite persuasively that both Kierkegaard's father, Michael Pedersen Kierkegaard, and Regine Olsen are likewise literary figures, poetized pseudonyms embodying powerful and conflicting forces active in Kierkegaard's own life: "sexuality and death, instinct and anguish, physical finitude and conscious freedom."[18] Michael Kierkegaard and Regine Olsen are indeed historical characters, but the information concerning their individual thoughts, perceptions, and actions is still quite limited, and much of it is colored by Søren Kierkegaard's statements concerning them. This lack once again makes it difficult to trace the transformation of a historical personage into a pseudonymic figure.

Lessing, then, is the only figure among the pseudonyms for whom fairly complete historical material is available: his own letters and other basically autobiographical information, his very extensive writings, and the comments, letters and written materials provided by contemporaries who associated with him in varying degrees of intimacy. Because of this extant material, it is possible to stand the historical and the pseudonymic Lessing back-to-back, to measure them against one another, and thereby to see how the two correspond, how they differ, what discrepancies may arise, and through this, what the "essence" of the pseudonym is. In other words, the treatment of Lessing shows how the pseudonyms differ from "reality." It illuminates the process by which an already existing standpoint or world-view is subtly molded and transformed as it enters the Kierkegaardian sphere. The Lessing pseudonym makes it possible to see what actually happens—this information can then be referred back to Socrates, Abraham, and the other pseudonymic figures.

Differences between Lessing and the Pseudonym

At this point, we will turn to the data presented in Section II, in an attempt to establish the exact form in which Lessing enters, or rather, leaps into the sphere of the pseudonyms. An analysis of the pseudonymic Lessing in relationship to the historical reveals a consistent pattern in those parts of the factual individual which are absorbed or distilled into the pseudonym.

Point #1 states: *Lessing is a subjectively existing thinker who, almost like Socrates, insures himself against fellowship and prevents discipleship.* In the section on Subjectivity it becomes clear that Lessing's historical position excludes him from true subjectivity in the Kierkegaardian sense. However, although at first glance it would seem that this quality cannot with justification be applied to the historical thinker, a closer investigation does, indeed, disclose a certain degree of incipient subjectivity in Lessing's life and work. Although he was not conscious of the individual as such, he was at the forefront of the awakening bourgeois consciousness of the middle-class as a valuable part of humanity. Even more important for Kierkegaard, Lessing demonstrates a striking degree of congruence between his life and his philosophy. The concepts of tolerance, humanity, understanding, and reason that he propounds in his writing also appear in concrete form in his actions and relationships with those around him. Both his work and his life are dedicated to a fearless search for truth, and a denunciation of all that he perceives to be false and hypocritical; and, through that which he writes, he attempts to educate the public, and to provoke them into thinking and forming their own judgements as well. As becomes clear in the course of the analysis, that which is of interest to Climacus is, therefore, not so much *what* Lessing says, since that is still limited by the bounds of his society and culture, as *how* he says it and, even more importantly, how he *reduplicates* his thought both in his writing and in his life. In this case, Kierkegaard/Climacus has stripped away historical limitation and presupposition, to reveal the purest essence of what he believes to be the motivating spirit behind the concrete facts, with which he then animates the Lessing pseudonym. In doing so, he focuses squarely on that which Lessing *is*, and the fact that his "philosophy is merely his life."

A similar situation occurs in respect to the God-relationship. Although his position was not so self-consciously and precisely stated as that of the pseudonym in the *Postscript*, the historical Lessing did demonstrate a sense of direct responsibility and accountability to God for his actions in his search for truth, and he refused to bend to the demands of any human being, be it his father or the pastor Goeze. He was very concerned with the actualization of religious belief in daily action. In addition, his driving search for truth served to isolate him from all the commonly accepted systems of belief and tradition that usually acted as the intermediary between God and humankind; that is, in his view religion should be a matter of direct personal involvement. In this sense, Kierkegaard/Climacus has again focused in on a trait genuine to the historical Lessing: Lessing *lived* a direct relationship with God, free of the mediation or opinions of others. As in the previous point, the essential concern is that Lessing's religious belief was "merely" his life—the emphasis is once more on Lessing's way of *being*. It must be noted, however, that a slight coloring has crept into the Lessing figure in the sense that, in the body of ideas that the historical Lessing recorded, there is no specific expression of an understanding that religion has to do only with the individual God-relationship, a trait that Climacus claims for the Lessing figure.

This type of creeping coloring or distortion appears even more clearly in the discussion of Discipleship. Although Climacus asserts that Lessing actively and consciously prevents discipleship, historical materials indicate that Lessing, because of his restless, questing spirit and his highly individual search for truth, quite simply fails to gain a coterie of followers. This occurs largely because particular characteristics of his personality, his attitude toward his work, his overriding desire to learn, and his flexible concept of truth serve as spontaneously alienating forces, which isolate him from any would-be followers and provide them little immediately graspable concrete doctrine. This illuminates very clearly one of the prime differences between factuality and ideality in the Lessing figures. That is, accidental historical facts and chains of historical cause and effect are meaningless in the ethereal sphere of the pseudonyms. In essence, Kierkegaard is not interested in *why* Lessing is as he is—the only matter of importance is that Lessing *is* as he is. The causal linkage within the historical context is entirely irrelevant to his purposes. In this, Kierkegaard remains within the range of what Lessing described as believability in a historical figure within a literary context. The element of distortion arises at the moment when Climacus imputes to Lessing a conscious decision to avoid or deter disciples; in other words, when that which occurs naturally, almost accidentally in the historical Lessing's work, becomes a matter of choice and conscious purpose in the pseudonym Lessing.

Point #2 reads: *[Lessing] through his silence and calculated withdrawal into himself, offers no results, develops no system, presents nothing which thoughtless adherents could repeat by rote.* The discussion of Lessing's silence establishes the fact that a certain degree of silence, both on the personal and on the tactical level, does indeed exist in many areas of Lessing's life and writings. Climacus, however, focuses solely on the religious—he sees only a man who, in an extraordinary manner refuses to betray the God-relationship and subjective religious experience that he has attained. In this case, Lessing's silence is clearly not Kierkegaard's silence, because the ideality that is projected into the Lessing figure contains something more than one could reasonably claim to have drawn from the historical Lessing. It is true that Lessing seems to equivocate or remain silent concerning the very points that would serve most to clarify exactly what his religious belief is. In light of the previous presentation, however, it becomes evident that his silence on this point is neither extraordinary nor significant. That is: on a personal level, Lessing habitually avoids direct discussion of all individual feelings, emotions, and convictions, not only in his publicly published works, but also in his private correspondence. He also refrains from such statements of personal content on a tactical level, partly because it is politically imprudent to do otherwise, and partly because the structure of his own polemic style precludes direct presentation of his own belief. In this respect, then, Climacus, as a result of his own subjective bias, has focused on one side of a trait essential to Lessing's personality and magnified it into an independent characteristic with significance in and of itself. And it is at this point that the reader begins to be somewhat suspicious of the Lessing pseudonym. According to Lessing, that which makes us able to accept fictionalized historical characters as "true" or genuine is not that they appear in exactly the same circumstances as would have been the case historically, but that their actions, thoughts, and sentiments coincide with our sense of what that particular character would have done, had he or she been in the type of situation described in the text in question. Thus, the level of consciousness and the religious bias previously mentioned seem to deviate in an inauthentic manner from the historical Lessing, who was interested in theological debate, but equally devoted to the exploration of philosophical, humanitarian, and aesthetic questions.

The section on Lessing's lack of system demonstrates that the German author's unsystematized output and absence of definitive results are, in reality, the natural product of the combined forces of Lessing's individual personality, his historical circumstances, and his polemic search for truth. However, as has been discussed, because Kierkegaard is interested in universal ideality, the historical "whys" that shaped Lessing's production have no real validity for him. He is concerned only with the fact that Lessing *did* it that way; but once again, this universalized Lessing, who has been freed from chains of historical cause and effect, is flavored by a degree of conscious decision that is clearly Kiergaardian rather than natural to Lessing.

Point #3 states: *[Lessing] communicates in an ironic form calculated to confuse and dismay the unwary.* The analysis of Lessing's style showed that although Lessing utilizes irony as a biting and devastating strategic weapon, he applies no specific philosophical connotations to it as a concept in and of itself. Irony seems to be such an integral and natural part of his style that it does not occur to him to separate it from himself and theorize about it. Although Lessing's style of communication did, indeed, often "confuse and dismay the unwary," Climacus steps far beyond any verifiable information on the historical Lessing, in that he insists that Lessing utilizes this combination of jest and earnestness as a conscious ploy designed to disguise true religious inwardness, so that only those who are existentially and subjectively involved can grasp it. Once again, then, a sense of conscious decision and calculation is introduced into the pseudonymic Lessing, exaggerating a trait that was spontaneous to the historical Lessing.

In summary, the Lessing figure in the *Postscript* is presented as the embodiment of the subjectively existing thinker who insures himself against fellowship and prevents discipleship. As has become clear through this analysis, there are, indeed, many points of greater or lesser congruence between the Lessing pseudonym and the historical individual. In filtering away the weight of historical factuality, Kierkegaard/Climacus focuses, above all, on Lessing's *being* itself. Through this emphasis on Lessing's essence rather than his writings, Kierkegaard is, in fact, following a direction of Lessing interpretation begun by the necrologist Johann Gottfried Herder at the time of Lessing's death in 1781, and intensified by Friedrich Schlegel, who insisted that Lessing himself was of more value than the sum of his talents.[19] It cannot be disputed that many inherent traits of Lessing's being, his personality, and his production—whatever their historical causes may have been—correspond remarkably well to Kierkegaard's concept of the subjectively existing individual. In particular, the historical Lessing does demonstrate an unusual unity of thought and existence. However, as has become clear in this discussion, the Lessing pseudonym is, not surprisingly, skewed or slanted in a particularly Kierkegaardian direction: toward the subjective and the religious. Still, although this is somewhat exaggerated in terms of Lessing's own reality, it does not strike the reader as being necessarily problematic. Lessing was extremely concerned with religious matters, and could, therefore, conceivably be imagined to think in the manner of the Lessing pseudonym. It is rather the element of conscious decision and driving purpose that makes up the greatest qualitative difference between the historical Lessing and the pseudonym—it is this distortive factor that leaves one with the uneasy impression that the familiar Lessing face is actually a mask worn by an unfamiliar spirit, in Lessing's terms, a "false person who has usurped a strange name and pretends to be what he is not" (*HD* 97).

Kierkegaard is acutely aware of the fact that both his existence and his production are governed by an intense reflective consciousness that predominates almost to the point of total exclusion of spontaneity. Because of this, all parts of his thought and style of writing become equally purposive and conscious, as if—to use Jean-François Marquet's metaphor—writing for him required the same agonizingly keen awareness as breathing would, were it to become something one must execute consciously, moment by moment, instead of being able to rely on the unconscious ability of the body. But writing and creative thought were, at the same time, as essential as breathing to Kierkegaard's survival as an individual,[20] a circumstance that drove him to exclaim "Blast it all, I can abstract from everything but *not from myself*; I cannot even forget myself when I sleep" (*JP* 5:69 #5142).

This sleepless consciousness, in turn, appears as one of the most striking characteristics of the various pseudonyms who inhabit the pages of the authorship. As Thompson states, the world of the pseudonyms is "the world of human consciousness itself, and its negativity."[21] What we find in the pseudonyms, then, is in fact "volatile human consciousness continually on the move."[22] Thus, as the mortal heaviness is stripped away from the historical Lessing, he, too, is transported from the sphere of immediacy to the level of reflection in which Climacus/Kierkegaard himself dwells. It is, therefore, almost to be expected that, in making this leap, as Lessing is filtered through Climacus' perception, the pseudonymic figure acquires a sense of searing subjective consciousness, which is further distorted by a single-minded religious bias. Because of this, every act, every statement, every characteristic of style is endowed with a penetrating reflective intent impossible to the historical Lessing's age. That which arose innately and spontaneously to the factual Lessing, even as the result of active creative effort on his part, becomes the fruit of conscious reflection and intent in the pseudonym Lessing. The natural by-products of Lessing's search for truth and enlightenment suddenly take on the significance of results consciously produced by a subjectively existing Lessing who does all in reference to his God-relationship. It is true that Climacus' depiction adds a universality to Lessing that would not be possible in a purely historical investigation. By divesting Lessing of accidental historical singularities, Climacus creates a symbol, a representation, an embodiment of a concept. This is not an idealization in the poetic sense—the irony of the presentation will not allow that. Rather, Climacus broadens the essence of the historical Lessing into universal application by abstracting the supra-individual from the actually individual. The result of this process, however, is that the familiar Lessing in the pages of the *Postscript* has an unfamiliar spirit. Although Kierkegaard, perhaps, believed that he had glimpsed the true Lessing behind the mask he wore, it would be necessary to assert that in the Lessing figure, one finds Lessing's ways used for Kierkegaard's means, both in Kierkegaard's struggle to find real Christianity and in his polemic against the Hegelians. The words, the actions are Lessing's own, but the spirit is something beyond him, the product of the sleepless Kierkegaardian consciousness.

This fact becomes very interesting in terms of Kierkegaard's assertion that he in actuality had "no connection" with the pseudonyms. In this context, perhaps Josiah Thompson's description of the pseudonyms as a prism refraction of Kierkegaard's own life[23] and being comes closest to an actual description of these figures. Although Kierkegaard claims that he had no role in determining the pseudonyms, that each, in fact, has his own essence and voice, the Lessing pseudonym shows that, to the contrary, even a figure that originally *did* have its own being and voice, comes to reflect the Kierkegaardian consciousness, and to speak, at least in part, in Kierkegaard's own voice as it enters the Kierkegaardian sphere. Perhaps Kierkegaard is correct in insisting that he—meaning his personal historical baggage—is entirely separate from the pseudonymic authors. However, the entire universe known to and peopled by the pseudonyms is the powerful, sleepless, acutely aware Kierkegaardian consciousness. If he is not the pseudonyms, then at least his consciousness is their world, the air they breathe, the blood in their veins, and it is impossible that even Lessing could enter here without becoming a native, without taking on something of the traits characteristic to the other inhabitants.

Why Lessing was Chosen

This point leads directly into the final question, that of why Lessing alone, out of all possible historical personalities, was chosen by Kierkegaard to be transformed into the pseudonym that appears in the *Postscript*. The answer is, perhaps, more simple than one might expect, although it is not entirely obvious. It is true that certain of Lessing's actions, personality traits, and characteristics of writing style seem to have drawn Kierkegaard's attention to the German thinker. But I would like to propose that the historical Lessing was distinguished by something of even greater significance to Kierkegaard: Lessing was chosen precisely because he *did* wear a mask—because the already existing ambiguity surrounding the historical Lessing was exactly suited to the Kierkegaardian needs. This would also help explain the presence in the authorship of other named figures whose history is equally ambivalent or obscure. As stated earlier, Kierkegaard was not at all interested in factual, scientific background or external historicity. He needed internal qualities that fit into the inescapable driving demands of his authorship—he needed figures from the past whose very names would call forth particular associations in the minds of the readers, and yet who were transparent enough already that their particular individuality would not cloud the ethereal refraction through the Kierkegaardian dynamo. It is most likely the case that if Lessing had been any less ambiguous as a historical individual, he would have been of little use to Kierkegaard, and would probably never have appeared among the pseudonyms.

Conclusion

In this insight, the question of why Lessing has been picked up and inserted into the heart of Kierkegaard's key philosophical tract finds an answer, as do the concerns expressed by critics such as Erik Lunding. To give visual concretion to the abstractions that he desires to present, Kierkegaard, as a sort of aesthetic shorthand, is in need of a figure whose very name is a symbol that will evoke certain preconnected ideas and impressions, a certain level of preconstructed understanding in the minds of his readers. If, however, he as an author were to proceed purely as a historian, if he were to limit himself to the concrete facts and truths operative in the historical Lessing's life, he would, in the end, possess nothing more than a socially and temporally limited individual; he could depict only how this particular person responded to this particular set of circumstances, and nothing more.

Instead, Kierkegaard goes about his work as would a dramatist or a novelist, who seeks to draw from the temporal individual that which has universal human application. As Lessing states, "Historical accuracy is not his aim, but only the means by which he hopes to attain his aim; he wishes to delude us and touch our hearts through this delusion" (*HD* 32). Lessing himself is merely a true case from the history book that happens to fit Kierkegaard's ends.

Much in the way described by Lessing in the *Dramaturgy*, Kierkegaard rejects all that is historically contingent, all concrete content as such. His desire seems to be to make visible the "passionate inwardness" that he senses as the motivating force behind Lessing's actions; he attempts to capture the quality of Lessing's being itself. In doing this, he is completely in harmony with Lessing's own conception of the way in which a historical figure is absorbed with believability into literature.

However, Kierkegaard is neither a dramatist nor a novelist. He insists constantly that his use of poetic or aesthetic form, his employment of characters or pseudonyms *per se* is not a function of sheer literary creativity. He does not write to be aesthetically pleasing to his readers, but rather to fulfill the needs of his overriding agenda, to drive readers into decisions about Christianity. What Kierkegaard desires in his pseudonyms is the concrete representation of various abstractions, rather than an assemblage of active personae. Therefore, because in Lessing Kierkegaard is not in any way attempting to present a rounded character, such as would be demanded by a novel or a drama, he can with impunity focus on certain traits to the total exclusion of others. Even this does not necessarily depart from the inner truth of the character. However, the end goals of the authorship demand something more; it is in response to his powerful need to illustrate authentic Christianity that Kierkegaard can take secondary and perhaps entirely spontaneous traits in the historical Lessing, and magnify them to prime importance in the pseudonymic Lessing. In doing this, of course, he begins to draw away from the inner truth of the Lessing figure as Lessing. In fact, the pseudonym begins to take on a new sort of inner truth—a pervading Kierkegaardian sort. This is even more strongly the case when it comes to the sense of acute consciousness and awareness, which, more than anything else, distinguishes the Lessing pseudonym from the historical Lessing.

It must always be remembered, however, that Kierkegaard, who is neither a historian, nor a dramatist, nor a novelist, is bound by no rules but his own. In fact, he is not looking for *the* Lessing—he is seeking *a* Lessing, there behind the mask of silence, ambiguity, and irony. And he in fact finds what he is looking for: a Lessing close enough to the historical man that certain ideas and preconceptions will still be automatically associated with the name, and yet pliable and transparent enough that he could successfully be filtered through the gauzy veil which divides the pseudonymic world from ours, that he could survive the sudden infusion of Kierkegaardian purpose and consciousness without ceasing to be himself altogether. Perhaps, in the end, it is only *because* he customarily appeared masked that Lessing can still be identified as Lessing, even within the Kierkegaardian sphere: the mask is Lessing's, even though the face behind it has come more closely to resemble the Dane.

Notes

Introduction

1. Søren Kierkegaard, *Concluding Unscientific Postscript*, trans. David F. Swenson [1941] (Princeton: Princeton University Press, 1968), 59. Subsequent citations from this work will be notated parenthetically in the text.

2. Søren Kierkegaard, *Søren Kierkegaard's Journals and Papers*, ed. and trans. Howard V. Hong and Edna H. Hong, 7 vols. (Bloomington: Indiana University Press, 1975), 2:518 #2240. Subsequent citations from these volumes will be notated parenthetically in the text.

3. Some examples of this procedure: In *JP* 1:425 #974, Kierkegaard admits a degree of truth in Lessing's idea that one essentially cannot admire the heroic, then goes on to develop his own view of the concept. In *JP* 3:28–29 #2377, Kierkegaard criticizes Lessing's tendency to write anonymously, then engages in a discussion of anonymity and authority. Further examples of Kierkegaard's criticism of Lessing, or his usage of Lessing's thought as a springboard into his own philosophy can be found in *JP* 3:30 #2379; *JP* 4:257 #4364; *JP* 4:266 #4375; and *JP* 4:304 #4474. In the period after the publication of the *Postscript*, as Kierkegaard turned increasingly to the directly religious, he became proportionately more critical of Lessing.

Chapter 1. Lessing's Actuality as a Pseudonymic Figure

1. The validity of the *Point of View* as an index to Kierkegaard's "actual intention" with the authorship has often been disputed. In this context, Louis Mackey's assertion in *Points of View: Readings of Kierkegaard* (Tallahassee: Florida State University Press, 1986), 190, that this volume presents, not *the* point of view, but *a* point of view for understanding the authorship can be instructive. As he insists:

> When a man fabricates as many masks to hide behind as Kierkegaard does, one cannot trust his (purportedly) direct asseverations. And when he signs his own name, it no longer has the effects of the signature.
>
> Soren Kierkegaard was one of his own pseudonyms. (Ibid., 188)

See also Niels Cappelørn, "The Retrospective Understanding of Søren Kierkegaard's Total Production," *Kierkegaard: Resources and Results*, Alastair McKinnon, ed. (Montreal, Ontario: Wilfrid Laurier University Press, 1982).

2. In this regard, see *JP* 5:226 #5645; 5:103 #5241; and 5:103 #5242.

3. In his work *Kierkegaard* (London: Routledge & Kegan Paul, 1982), 57, Alastair Hannay states:

> By transferring ownership of the works and their prefaces to fictitious authors Kierkegaard has acquired a combination, so to speak, of the reporter's freedom from having to answer personally for the views he passes on, and of the fiction-writer's freedom to create the persons (and perspectives) of whom (and which) the views are expressions. The advantages of this for someone who wants the views to take effect without consideration of their author's real intentions are obvious.

4. For specific references in this regard, see *JP* 4:229 #4312 and *JP* 4:232 #4315.

5. Walter Kaufmann, "Kierkegaard," *The Kenyon Review* 18:2 (Spring 1956): 208. It must be observed at this point that not all critics agree with this view of Kierkegaardian psychology and style. In this respect, Josiah Thompson protests in *Kierkegaard* (London: Victor Gollancz Ltd., 1974):

> This, I suspect, is precisely the aim of the pseudonyms: not to get the reader to make some impossible "existential movements," but to make the point that all such attempts at self-direction must fail. It is *failure*, I submit, the necessary failure of all human projects, that is the central meaning of the pseudonyms, as well as the source of their deepest religious import. (185)

Thompson then continues:

> It is God who ultimately haunts the world of the pseudonyms. He lurks not in their words, but between their words, in their silences and failures. Theirs is an ambience of duplicity and illusion. They are tricksters and playactors, speaking evasively and ironically. (Ibid., 186)

Thompson's conclusion:

> What the pseudonyms illustrate is the failure of all attempts to prevent our lives boiling off into the imaginary. Like us, the pseudonyms never succeed in becoming integral, never overcome a fundamental dissipation. Yet precisely in that failure can be glimpsed, ambiguously, like a shape half-seen in a mirror, the face of God. (Ibid., 187)

6. Kaufmann, "Kierkegaard," 208–9.

7. Poul Lübcke, "Kierkegaard and Indirect Communication," *History of European Ideas* 12.1 (1990): 32.

8. Ibid., 35.

9. Bernard Zelechow, "Fear and Trembling and Joyful Wisdom—The Same Book: A Look at Metaphoric Communication," *History of European Ideas* 12.1 (1990): 94.

10. Robert C. Roberts, *Faith, Reason, and History: Rethinking Kierkegaard's "Philosophical Fragments"* (Macon, Ga.: Mercer University Press, 1986), 2.

See similar observations in Mark Taylor, *Kierkegaard's Pseudonymous Authorship: A Study of Time and the Self*, (Princeton: Princeton University Press, 1975), 58: "the movement of the pseudonymous works is always away from the author and toward the reader. In writing the pseudonymous works Kierkegaard seeks to withdraw his own person as far as possible from his works." Additionally, Bertel Pederson, in his article "Fictionality and Authority: A Point of View for Kierkegaard's Work as an Author," in *Søren Kierkegaard*, ed. Harold Bloom (New York: Chelsea House Publishers, 1989), 105, states: "The effect of this method is to remove each text further from the writer who wrote it, emphasizing a distance as well as an ironical structure and status."

Frederick Sontag concludes in "Strange Interlude," *Man and World* 21.2 (Mar.

1988): 213, that Kierkegaard "intentionally wrote so that no interpretation, not even his own, could be authoritative or final. Should such be possible, it would take away the responsibility from the reader for his decision and subjective appropriation."

Refer to Pat Bigelow, *Kierkegaard and the Problem of Writing* (Tallahassee: The Florida State University Press, 1987) for a complex and thorough analysis of "the deconstructive force of Kierkegaard's 'indirect communication'" (Ibid., 3).

11. Eliyahu Rosenow, in "Kierkegaard's Mirror," *Educational Philosophy and Theory* 22.1 (1990): 11, agrees that "indirect communication sets up a screen between Kierkegaard and 'his' reader. . . .The indirect form . . . preserves the distance that must be maintained between the teacher and the pupil." John W. Elrod, in *Being and Existence in Kierkegaard's Pseudonymous Works*, (Princeton: Princeton University Press, 1975), 6, similarly comments on "Kierkegaard's demonic delight in confusing his reader," and continues, "He deliberately goes out of his way to make it difficult to understand him, and he has warned us that the most obvious routes into his writings are most likely not the correct ones."

12. Martin Thust, "Das Marionettentheater Sören Kierkegaards," *Zeitwende* 1 (1925): 18–38.

13. Walter Lowrie, "Editor's Introduction" to Søren Kierkegaard's *Repetition*, trans. Walter Lowrie (Princeton: Princeton University Press, 1946), xi. Subsequent citations from this work will be notated parenthetically in the text.

14. See "A First and Last Declaration" in *CUP*. The same ideas occur frequently in the journals. For example, see *JP* 6:177–78 #6440 and *JP* 6:428–29 #6786.

15. Pierre Mesnard, *Le Vrai Visage de Kierkegaard* (Paris: Beauchesne et ses Fils, 1948), 87.

16. Stephen Crites, "Pseudonymous Authorship as Art and as Act," *Kierkegaard: A Collection of Critical Essays*, ed. Josiah Thompson (Garden City, N.Y.: Anchor Books–Doubleday & Co., Inc., 1972), 215–16.

17. Georges Gusdorf, *Kierkegaard* (Paris: Éditions Seghers, 1963), 76–77.

18. Michael Plekon, "'Anthropological Contemplation': Kierkegaard and Modern Social Theory," *Thought: A Review of Culture and Idea* 55.218 (Sept. 1980): 349.

19. Henning Fenger, "Kierkegaard as a Falsifier of History," *Søren Kierkegaard*, ed. Harold Bloom (New York: Chelsea House Publishers, 1989), 168, 167.

20. Josiah Thompson, *Kierkegaard* (London: Victor Gollancz Ltd., 1974), 139, 142.

21. Søren Kierkegaard *Stages on Life's Way*, trans. Walter Lowrie (Princeton: Princeton University Press, 1945), esp. 21, 24. Subsequent citations from this work will be notated parenthetically in the text.

22. Søren Kierkegaard, *The Concept of Dread*, trans. Walter Lowrie [1944] (Princeton: Princeton University Press, 1967), 5–6.

23. Søren Kierkegaard, *Fear and Trembling and The Sickness unto Death*, trans. Walter Lowrie [1941] (Princeton: Princeton University Press, 1968), 23–24.

24. A few examples: (a) A's papers contain a thorough analysis and critique of Johannes the Seducer in the beginning of "The Diary," Søren Kierkegaard, *Either/Or*, trans. David F. Swenson and Lillian Marvin Swenson, 2 vols. [1944] (Princeton: Princeton University Press, 1971), 1:299–308. (Subsequent references to this work will be notated parenthetically in the text.) (b) Victor Eremita corrects Judge William's misquotes and miscalculations (*EO* 1:11). (c) Frater Taciturnus in *Stages* analyzes Constantine's similar thought experiment in *Repetition*, admitting that there are certain points of Constantine's approach which he cannot understand, then going on to compare his Quidam with Constantine's young man (*SLW* 366–67). (d) Constantine's young man levels a passionate load of criticism at his mentor and creator, while

Constantine presents his somewhat defensive view and criticism of the young man (young man: *R* 97–98; Constantine *R* 82–84). (e) William Afham gives a rather complete assessment of the young man and the Ladies' Tailor (*SLW* 37–38). (f) As previously mentioned, Climacus gives a lengthy review of the others (including Kierkegaard himself) in *CUP* 225–66.

25. It is significant that the Frater, in reference to the female counterpart to his Quidam, states that "By equipping her differently I should . . . have prevented my chief character from being adequately illuminated" (*SLW* 365).

26. In reference to the idea of being *aufgehoben* (transcended) it is instructive to note Stephen Crites' analysis in "Pseudonymous Authorship," 216–17. Crites states that most of the pseudonyms are situated in a definite point-of-view, and represent "animated life-possibilities." However, in his opinion:

> in every case the point of view from which the work is written is itself transcended within the work, "*aufgehoben*" or at least rendered problematical, its limitations revealed. And yet that *aufgehoben* point of view, the possibility represented by the pseudonymous author, is the standpoint from which the whole problem of the work is treated. Every pseudonym occupies a specific position which like a mirror reflects its problem according to its angle of vision. . . . Every scheme or problem treated earlier is transformed when Kierkegaard projects his imagination into the frame of another pseudonym. And any existential movement treated in a particular work is presented as it is viewed from the pseudonymous author's angle of vision, generally glimpsed as it moves out of his field of vision altogether.

27. Søren Kierkegaard, *Philosophical Fragments*, trans. David F. Swenson and Howard V. Hong [1936] (Princeton: Princeton University Press, 1967), 6–7. Subsequent citations from this work will be notated parenthetically in the text.

28. Kierkegaard comments extensively on his relationship with ideality and the ideal, as, for example, in *JP* 6:400–401 #6749 and *JP* 6:336 #6650.
Stephen Crites, in "Pseudonymous Authorship," 210, points out the working of the aesthetic mode in this consideration:

> The ideality bodied forth in a work of art is always an abstraction from experience. It arises out of the temporality of experience, but it achieves a purified form as a self-contained possibility, free of temporality. That is why both the artist and his audience are able to come to rest in it. At least for this ideal moment of experience a man achieves integration, his consciousness drawn together by its concentration on a single purified possibility.

29. Paul L. Holmer, "Post-Kierkegaard: Remarks about Being a Person," *Kierkegaard's Truth: The Disclosure of the Self*, ed. Joseph H. Smith (New Haven: Yale University Press, 1981), 13. Note also Mark C. Taylor's description of the pseudonyms as "ideal personality types. By 'ideal' Kierkegaard means that these life-views are never found in as pure a form in actual existence as they are in their pseudonymous representatives" (Taylor, *Pseudonymous Authorship*, 55). In the same sense, M. Holmes Hartshorne states in *Kierkegaard Godly Deceiver: The Nature and Meaning of his Pseudonymous Writings* (New York: Columbia University Press, 1990), 26, that the alternatives presented in *Either/Or* are "*extremes that can be thought, but they cannot be lived.*"

30. See the extensive statement concerning the role of Governance in Kierkegaard's authorship in the *Point of View*.

31. Richard Campbell, "Lessing's Problem and Kierkegaard's Answer," *Scottish Journal of Theology* (Edinburgh) 19.1 (1966): 35–54.

32. Jacques Colette, "Kierkegaard et Lessing," *Revue des Sciences Philosophiques et Théologiques* 44 (1960): 3–39.

33. Gordon E. Michalson, Jr.: (a) "Lessing, Kierkegaard and the 'Ugly Ditch': a Reexamination," *Journal of Religion* 59.3 (1979): 324–34; (b) *Lessing's "Ugly Ditch": A Study of Theology and History* (University Park and London: The Pennsylvania State University Press, 1985); and (c) "Kierkegaard's Debt to Lessing: Response to Whisenant," *Modern Theology* 6.4 (July 1990): 379–84.

34. James Whisenant, "Kierkegaard's Use of Lessing," *Modern Theology* 6.3 (April 1990): 259–72.

35. Paul Requadt, "Lessing, Schlegel, Kierkegaard," *Neue Schweizer Rundschau* 36/37 (1929): 103–8.

36. Claus von Bormann, "Kierkegaard und Lessing," *Kierkegaard und die deutsche Philosophie seiner Zeit*, Hsg. Heinrich Anz, Peter Kemp, und Friedrich Schmöe (München: Wilhelm Fink Verlag, 1980).

37. Hans-Martin Gerlach, "Wahrheit und Geschichte/Lessing oder Kierkegaard?" *Lessing-Konferenz, Halle 1979*, Hsg. Hans-Georg Werner, Teil 2 (Halle [Saale]: Martin-Luther-Universität Wissenschaftliche Beiträge, 1980).

38. Erik Lunding, "Lessing und Kierkegaard," *Orbis Litterarum* 2 (1944): 158–87.

39. Lunding, "Lessing," 173.

40. Ibid., 178.

41. Ibid., 184.

42. Ibid., 186.

43. Ibid., 187.

44. The relationship of history and ideality and the validity of historical data is discussed further in the section on "Abstracting a Historical Figure into a Pseudonym."

45. Jacques Colette in "Kierkegaard" partakes in this same confusion when he isolates the three major themes in Kierkegaard's Lessing admiration as (1) Double reflection and the subjectively existing thinker, (that is, the Lessing figure); (2) historical revelation and eternal bliss, the concept of the "leap," (that is, the theses attributable to Lessing); and (3) truth and objectivity (once again, the theses). Colette experiences much of the same difficulty as Lunding in justifying Kierkegaard's relationship to Lessing, since he, too, refers to the historical Lessing rather than the pseudonymous ideality.

46. The extensive Climacus quote set off with dots is taken entirely from *CUP* 60.

Chapter 2. How the Pseudonymic and Historical Lessing Figures Correspond and Differ

1. See, for example, *JP* 4:157 #4157 and *JP* 5:294 #5842.

2. Søren Kierkegaard, *The Point of View for my Work as an Author*, trans. Walter Lowrie (New York: Harper Torchbooks–Harper and Row, Publishers, 1962), 130. (All subsequent references to this work will be notated parenthetically in the text.)
For information on the "modern age" and the modernization of Denmark, see John W. Elrod, *Kierkegaard and Christendom* (Princeton: Princeton University Press, 1981); and Bruce H. Kirmmse, *Kierkegaard in Golden Age Denmark* (Bloomington & Indianapolis: Indiana University Press, 1990).

3. Plekon, "Contemplation," 358.

4. Ibid., 356.

5. Merold Westphal, *Kierkegaard's Critique of Reason and Society* (Macon, Ga.: Mercer University Press, 1987), 43.

6. David Bruce Fletcher, *Social and Political Perspectives in the Thought of Soren Kierkegaard* (Washington, D.C.: University Press of America, 1982), 51.

7. Westphal, *Critique*, 34.

8. Ibid., 44.

9. Ibid.

10. See the discussion in Plekon, "Contemplation," 358–59.

11. Westphal, *Critique*, 34.

12. Fletcher, *Perspectives*, 47.

13. Among numerous references, see particularly *JP* 2:401 #2004 in this respect.

14. C. Stephen Evans, "Kierkegaard on Subjective Truth: Is God an Ethical Fiction?" *International Journal for Philosophy of Religion* 7.1 (1976): 291.

15. See, for example, the discussion by Indu Jalota in "Kierkegaard's Notion of Subjectivity and its Bearing on the Problem of Communication," *Indian Philosophical Quarterly* 7 (April 1980): 393–94:

> Subjectivity is interpreted in terms of passionate inwardness which represents personal concern and involvement. . . . Truth is not something that is outside the individual as an end-product. It is to be assimilated in inwardness. The subjective thinker is concerned first with his own existence and everything else in relation to himself. Without this human or existential relationship, the objects of the world have no significance, thus everything external has to be transformed into things internal and each such act constitutes an affirmation of subjectivity.

Concerning the statement "truth is subjectivity," Michael Galati, in "A Rhetoric for the Subjectivist in a World of Untruth: the Tasks and Strategy of Soren Kierkegaard," *The Quarterly Journal of Speech* 55 (1969): 373, asserts:

> Of course, [Kierkegaard] is not here referring to phenomenal truths or truths ordinarily derived from sense observations. Such truth, to Kierkegaard, is indifferent to one's existence. He speaks rather of truth as "essential" truth, or about "truth which is essentially related to existence," which, because of its essential relationship to existence, would not be separable from the existing examiner. He is speaking, of course, of religious truths or of truths ordinarily discussed under the heading of metaphysics. . . .To Kierkegaard it is exactly this subjectivity that is truth. It concerns the *how* rather than the *what*.

Along this same line, see the discussion by Richard Schacht in "Kierkegaard on 'Truth is Subjectivity' and 'The Leap of Faith.'" *Canadian Journal of Philosophy* 2.3 (March 1973): 301, where he clarifies that, in relationship to truth, it is important:

> not that one simply come to *know* what one's essential nature *qua* human being is, but rather that one *actualize* it, by achieving the appropriate inner state.

George J. Stack's article, "The Meaning of 'Subjectivity is Truth'," *Midwest Journal of Philosophy* (Spring 1975): 26–40, also provides useful insight regarding this question.

16. Fletcher, *Perspectives*, 1.

17. Earl McLane, "Kierkegaard and Subjectivity," *International Journal for Philosophy of Religion* 8.4 (1977): 213–14. Also instructive in the context of Kierkegaard's social consciousness are John W. Elrod, "The Social Dimension of Despair," *International Kierkegaard Commentary: "The Sickness unto Death"* (Macon, Ga.: Mercer University Press, 1987); and Bruce H. Kirmmse, "Psychology and Society: The Social Falsification of the Self in *The Sickness unto Death*," *Kierkegaard's Truth: The Disclosure of the Self*, ed. Joseph H. Smith (New Haven: Yale University Press, 1981).

18. Schacht, "Truth is Subjectivity," 302.

19. Westphal, *Critique*, 47.
20. Fletcher, *Perspectives*, 67.
21. Ibid., 52.
22. See, for example, the statement in *JP* 3:651 #3587. Note also the assertion in Louis Mackey, "The Poetry of Inwardness," *Kierkegaard: A Collection of Critical Essays*, ed. Josiah Thompson (Garden City, N.Y.: Anchor Books–Doubleday & Co., Inc., 1972), 71, that in the Kierkegaardian sense:

> A human being is a freedom caught in the intersection of time and eternity, there constrained to mold in decision and action the integrity, the existing truth at once actual and ideal, that he does not have by nature and cannot find by taking thought.

23. Fletcher, *Perspectives*, 66.
24. Ibid.
25. Ibid.
26. Ibid.
27. See the references to this idea in *JP* 6:370–71 #6716; *JP* 1:265 #646; *JP* 6:37 #6224; *JP* 1:460 #1056; *JP* 3:701 #3673; and *JP* 3:606 #3519.
28. See, for example, *JP* 3:152 #2640; *JP* 4:360 #4564; *JP* 3:487–88 #3223; and *JP* 3:488 #3224.
29. See the explanation in Jalota, "Subjectivity," 393:

> Kierkegaard's philosophy is opposed to all conceptual schemes and theoretical systems. A theoretical enquiry into the nature of human existence would ignore the reality of man and reduce him to a mere object. Indeed, the very starting-point of Kierkegaard's philosophy takes the form of protest against such systematisation and objectification. The subjective dimension of human existence as analyzed by Kierkegaard defies categorisation. This is the significance of his characterising human existence as subjectivity in contrast to the objectivity of the speculative modes of thought and of science. . . .The self has its original being, its true actuality in what cannot be stated as an objective event.

30. Schacht, "Truth is Subjectivity," 307.
31. As Richard Schacht describes this phenomenon in "Truth is Subjectivity," 299, Kierkegaard feels that his contemporaries, especially the intellectuals, seem to believe that human beings are to be viewed mainly as *knowers*, and that the attainment of knowledge is their most important capacity. To attain knowledge, however, one must have an attitude of objectivity, which can only be acquired through suppressing personality and transcending individuality. In this attempt to abandon one's personality and individuality, Kierkegaard "sees a kind of self-annihilation to which he objects in the strongest possible terms." In the face of this tendency, the Dane asserts that "men are essentially finite, subjective, particular individuals, rather than unlimited, objective, impersonal knowing spirits."
See also the excellent discussion of this topic in Robert C. Roberts, "Thinking Subjectively," *International Journal for the Philosophy of Religion* 11 (Summer 1980): 71–92.
32. See Kierkegaard's characterization of this state in *JP* 3:522 #3317. In this respect, Robert C. Roberts points out in "Thinking Subjectively," 77, that:

> When Kierkegaard says that ethics is the one thing lacking in Hegel's system he of course does not mean that ethical concepts do not get discussed there. What he means is that they are discussed in such a way as to leave out an essential aspect of them . . . namely their character as self-implicating in the mouth of any person who uses them. For Hegel uses them in the interest of a kind of pure

"science," the self-adequate alignment of thoughts with one another into a system. As such, this use of ethical concepts divorces them from reference to any human individual, including Hegel and his reader, and so the ethical concepts cease to be ethical by being cut off from the soil which is their homeland.

33. In this respect, see also *JP* 4:350 #4548.

34. Wilfried Barner, Gunter Grimm, Helmuth Kiesel, and Martin Kramer, eds., *Lessing: Epoche—Werk—Wirkung* (München: C. H. Beck'sche Verlagsbuchhandlung, 1975), 41, presents a concise and yet thorough discussion of the political and social relationships prevalent during the period of the Enlightenment in Germany. Among other points mentioned are the fact that the princes and sovereigns reigned as the patriarchal authority in the state, while the subjects were treated as minors who lacked the ability to decide for themselves what was good and helpful for them, and what was detrimental.

35. For further discussion of the relationship between the private and public spheres and the incipient privatization of which Lessing was a part, see, for example, Hinrich C. Seeba, *Die Liebe zur Sache: Öffentliches und privates Interesse in Lessings Dramen* (Tübingen: Max Niemeyer Verlag, 1973), esp. 115–17; and Volker Nölle, *Subjektivität und Wirklichkeit in Lessings dramatischem und theologischem Werk* (Berlin: Erich Schmidt Verlag, 1977), esp. 271–78.

36. Lessing's description, in *Hamburg Dramaturgy*, trans. Helen Zimmern (New York: Dover Publications, Inc., 1962), 154 is as follows:

> Fine sentences and moral maxims are just what we are likely to hear least from a philosopher like Sokrates, his life was the only moral that he preached. But what we learn in his society is to know man and ourselves; to be observant of our emotions; to search for and to love the smoothest and shortest paths of nature; to judge each matter according to its intention.

(Subsequent citations from this work will be notated parenthetically in the text.)

37. A more extensive discussion of Lessing's concept of theater versus history appears in Section 3, "Abstracting a historical Figure into a Pseudonym." See also Lessing's comments in *Gotthold Ephraim Lessings sämtliche Schriften*, Karl Lachmann und Franz Muncker, Hsg., 3. Aufl., 23 Bände (Leipzig: G.J. Göschen'sche Verlagshandlung, 1904), 9: 227–28, 9:281–84, 9:315–16, 9:324–25 and 10:168–69. Subsequent references to these works will be notated parenthetically in the text.

38. Hans Mayer, in "Lessings poetische Ausdrucksform," *Lessing und die Zeit der Aufklärung* (Göttingen: Vandenhoeck & Ruprecht, 1968), 135, points out that Lessing's works contain no trace of the desire to present his own life and work autobiographically. Unlike Goethe, Lessing has no interest in seeing himself historically, and he avoids anything which could be called poetic self-presentation: Lessing presents no transformation of his own experience on stage, and at no time treats his work as a vehicle for finding the self. Nathan, for example, is not Lessing—he is merely a means of presenting Lessing's thoughts. Rather than a poetic self-revelation, the dramatic poem is a forum for continuing the debate with Goeze.

39. Klaus Briegleb discusses the difficulties involved in Lessing's biography in *Lessings Anfänge 1742–1746. Zur Grundlegung kritischer Sprachdemokratie* (Frankfurt: Athenäum Verlag, 1971), 30–32.

40. It is worth noting that this approach to Lessing places Kierkegaard very close to Friedrich Schlegel's assertion in *Kritische Friedrich-Schlegel-Ausgabe*, Ernst Behler, Hsg., 35 Bände (Paderborn: Verlag Ferdinand Schöningh, 1967), 2:112. *"He himself was of more value than all his talents.* In his uniqueness lay his greatness."

41. Ruth K. Angress, "Reflections on Lessing's Style and Manner as a Critic," *Lessing in heutiger Sicht*, Edward P. Harris und Richard E. Schade, Hsg. (Bremen: Jaco-

bi Verlag, 1977), 224. Other sources of particular interest in relationship to Lessing's criticism are Horst Steinmetz, "Der Kritiker Lessing: Zu Form und Methode der *Hamburgischen Dramaturgie*," *Neophilologus* 52 (1968): 30–48; Ernst Keller, *Kritische Intelligenz, G. E. Lessing, F. Schlegel, L. Borne* (Bern: Herbert Lang, 1976); and Barner, *Epoche*, esp. 119–21.

42. Further insight into Lessing's relationship to authority is provided by Steven D. Martinson in "Authority and Criticism: Lessing's Critical and Dramatic Procedure," *Humanität und Dialog*, Ehrhard Bahr, Edward P. Harris und Laurence G. Lyon, Hsg. (Detroit: Wayne State University Press, 1982), 143–54.

43. The fact that Lessing would consider a good character to be of importance to a successful writer (whose task it is to work toward the enlightenment of humanity and the demolition of falsehood) lends further credence to the idea that Lessing did in fact display a certain subjectivity in the Kierkegaardian sense in his thought and life.

See also Peter Michelsen, "Der Kritiker des Details: Lessing in den 'Briefen die Neueste Literatur betreffend'," *Wolfenbütteler Studien zur Aufklärung* 2 (1975): esp. 166–68.

44. A classic example of this would be Lessing's famed denunciation of Gottsched, particularly in the 17th *Literaturbrief* (Letters on Literature). In addition, much of Lessing's criticism of the French arises from his claim that they had mistranslated and misunderstood Aristotle. In the same vein, Lessing accuses Goeze of misreading and misinterpreting various biblical passages.

45. In addition, note Lessing's recommendation in *LS* 8:50:

> However, changes and corrections which a poet such as Friedrich Gottlieb Klopstock makes in his works, deserve not only to be noticed, but also to be studied with all diligence. One studies in them the most refined rules of art; because that which the masters of art deem worthy of observation, these are rules.

In relationship to the writing of tragedy, he admonishes:

> One should not start working before he is for the most part sure of his subject! And when is this possible? When one has studied Nature, when one has studied the Ancients enough. But this is a long apprenticeship! (*LS* 8:216)

In the same vein, Lessing delivers this advice to Karl:

> I have told you verbally often enough, where I believe you to be lacking. You have too little philosophy, and work much too carelessly. In order to make the viewers laugh in such a way that they do not laugh at us simultaneously, one must have studied very earnestly for a long while. (*LS* 17:294 #234)

See also *LS* 17:348 #279.

46. Hans Mayer, "Lessing und Aristoteles," *Festschrift für Bernhard Blume*, Hsg. Egon Schwarz, Hunter G. Hannum und Edgar Lohner (Göttingen: Vandenhoeck & Ruprecht, 1967), 62.

47. Barner, *Epoche*, 120–21.

48. Angress, "Reflections," 227. Wilhelm Mummenhoff, in "Die Darstellungsweise Lessings in seinen prosaischen Schriften," *73. Jahresbericht des Gymnasiums zu Recklinghausen Schuljahr 1902–1903* (Recklinghausen: J. Bauer, 1903), 9, illustrates Lessing's manner of presenting truth in this way:

> This manner of delivery transplants, as Engel expresses it, the truth into the soul of the reader in the same way in which it has grown in the author's own soul; it gives him not merely the chopped off, barren trunk, but rather the entire plant with its roots and a bit of clinging earth, so that it can proliferate vitally within the reader.

49. See the well-known discussion of truth in the *Duplik* (Defendant's Rejoinder) (*LS* 13:22–24). For a more detailed discussion of Lessing's conception of truth, see also Klaus Bohnen, "Aspekte marxistischer Lessing-Rezeption. (Mehring, Lukács, Rilla)," *Das Bild Lessings in der Geschichte*, Herbert G. Göpfert, Hsg. (Heidelberg: Verlag Lambert Schneider, 1981): esp. 1–2; and Barner, *Epoche*, esp. 267–73.

50. Lessing's assessment of mediocre works:

> we are merely saying, that [such works] at the present time have all produced something good, in a certain way and at a certain level. These times for the most part have been the childhood of our good taste. Children need milk, not heavy nourishment. From Weise to Haller would have been much too great a leap, and this rapid change could perhaps have been just as dangerous to good taste as it would be to a child, whom, immediately after milk, one would like to accustom to strong wine. Therefore, were not those works also necessary, that were just as far beneath the one, as above the others? At least for the masses, who are able to better themselves only step by step. In this manner, the admirers have multiplied, and many a mind has been encouraged, which perhaps would have been deterred by nothing but masterpieces. (*LS* 4:49–50)

51. A few quotes chosen from many: (a) The witty and the unwitty can parrot the comical; but only the heart can capture the language of the heart. It has its own rules; and it is all over with it, at the moment when one fails to realize this, and wishes instead to subject it to the rules of grammar, and to give it all the cold completeness, all the tedious distinctness which we demand in a logical sentence (*LS* 9:265). (b) Why do we not praise Plautus, whose servants think and speak as servants could think and speak? And why do we not censure Marivaux, whose servants are certainly servants, but servants from a marivaux-ian world, never from ours? (*LS* 4:183).
See also the critique of pompous language in *LS* 9:266; 10:31–32; and 8:145, as well as the criticism of Dusch, whose poetic hero, a miserable fisherman, speaks "naturally, like the poet Dusch" (*LS* 8:108). To actors, Lessing admonishes:

> All maxims must come from the abundance of the heart, with which the mouth overflows. We must appear to have thought of them as little as we intend to boast of them.

The piece continues with a plea for natural accent in speech, rather than false affectation, which might lead the listeners to suspect that the actors do not understand what they are saying (*HD* 12). Similar comments occur in *HD* 8.
A thorough discussion of Lessing's usage of language, and his demand for naturalness is found in Keller, *Intelligenz*.

52. For further discussion of Lessing's dramatic method in this context, see: (1) Steven D. Martinson, "The Cunning of Deceit in Lessing's Major Works," *Lessing Yearbook 14* (München: Max Hueber Verlag, 1982): 99–118; (2) Paul Böckmann, "Das Formprinzip des Witzes bei Lessing," *Gotthold Ephraim Lessing*, Gerhard Bauer und Sibylle Bauer, Hsg. (Darmstadt: Wissenschaftliche Buchgesellschaft, 1968): 176–95; (3) Walter Jens, "Feldzüge eines Redners. Gotthold Ephraim Lessing," *Von deutscher Rede* (München: R. Piper & Co. Verlag, 1969): esp. 60 ff.; and (4) Keller, *Intelligenz*.

53. To cite a few of Lessing's most important statements in this respect: (a) What do I care about the orthodox [hierarchy]? I despise them just as much as you do; however, I despise our new-fangled clerics even more, who are much too inept as theologians and yet far from being philosophers. I am also convinced of such insipid minds, that, if one were to allow them to ascend, in time they would tyrannize more than the orthodox [hierarchy] ever has (*LS* 18:83 #387). (b) I hate all people who desire to

found sects, from the depths of my heart. It is not error, but rather sectarian error, yes, even sectarian truth, that creates mankind's unhappiness; or would do it, if the truth desired to found a sect (*LS* 18:109 #408). (c) it [is] indeed basically true, that my theological—as you like to call it—banter or squabbles, have more to do with common sense than theology, and only for that reason do I prefer the old orthodox (basically tolerant) theology to the newer (basically intolerant) theology, because the former openly disputes with common sense, and the latter would prefer to bribe it. I get along with my open enemies, so that I can be better on guard against the secret ones (*LS* 18:226–27 #546).

54. The entire quote:

> Oh you fools! who would like to banish the gale from nature, because it buries a ship in a sandbar there, and here dashes another to pieces against the rocky shore!—Oh you hypocrites! for we know you. You are not concerned about these unfortunate ships, or else you would have made them secure: you are concerned solely about your own tiny garden; about your own small comfort, your little amusement. The malicious gale! there it has unroofed your summer-house; there shaken the laden trees too much; there overturned your entire costly orangery, in seven earthen pots. What do you care, how much good the gale otherwise promotes in nature? Could it not promote it without harming your little garden? Why doesn't it blow on past your fence? or at least fill its cheeks less full, at the moment it arrives at your boundary-stones? (*LS* 13:158–59)

55. For interesting insight into the subjective nature of Lessing's relationshp to truth in the context of the theological debates, see Helmut Thielicke, "Lessing und Goeze," *Text + Kritik* 26/27 (1970): 39–52.

56. (a) See, for example, Lessing's critique of the term *Hausplage* (a cantankerous marriage partner, almost entirely used in reference to a woman) as something considered to be obviously and self-evidently feminine (*LS* 17:352 #282). (b) Lessing's reaction to the Grenadier can be found particularly in *LS* 17:158 #110 and 17:155 #108. (c) In spite of the fact that he criticizes the shallowness and corruption among the nobility, Lessing, nevertheless, demonstrates a far more understanding and realistic attitude toward the nobles than was usually the case. For example, the statement concerning the noble class in general:

> They are all nothing more than quite ordinary people; and I am just as wrong if I hold them to be tigers and foxes, as others are, who make them into angels (*LS* 18:104 #405).

Lessing also tends to demonstrate a more accepting attitude toward the *Volk* (the common people) or *Pöbel* (rabble, the masses) than was usually the case. See the examples in *LS* 13:161ff., and particularly, 18:26–27 #353.
In addition, Agnes Heller, in "Aufklärung gegen Fundamentalismus: Der Fall Lessing," *Lessing Yearbook 19* (Detroit: Wayne State University Press, 1988), presents important insight into Lessing's relationship to many of the intolerant attitudes prevalent at his time.

See also Gisela F. Ritchie, *Der Dichter und die Frau* (Bonn: Bouvier Verlag, 1989); and Beate Sturges, *Lessing als Wegbereiter der Emanzipation der Frau* (New York: Peter Lang, 1989).

57. (a) The examples of this type of criticism are numerous. See for instance *LS* 10:200–201 in which Lessing criticizes the assumed rule that the evildoer in a comedy must either be punished or reformed at the end. (b) In *LS* 9:377–78, Lessing points out the absurdities created by the attempt to strictly enforce the unities of place and time exactly as the ancients did. (c) *LS* 10:29–31 discusses the absurdities produced by the

continued implementation of bombastic, stylized language. (d) *LS* 9:273–75 points out the foolishness of overstrict adherence to the unity of time.

58. See also *LS* 9:250.

59. One of the most notable examples of this battle imagery is to be found in *LS* 13:21, in which Lessing describes his role in the Reimarus debate as that of a *Kampfwärtel* (referee in a game of war). Similarly, in 13:181, Lessing employs the terminology of fencing as he speaks of driving the pastor into a corner. In 13:149 he describes his style as a sword that wounds. *LS* 17:255 #200 mentions his declaration of war on Klotz. *LS* 18:292 #617 characterizes *Nathan* as a means of making a flank attack. In 18:265 #594, Lessing describes his debate with Goeze in terms of light troops, main army, etc.

60. The particular characteristics of Lessing's style of writing are discussed in greater depth at a later point in this section.

61. For references to divine intervention in Lessing's life, see among others *LS* 17:41 #34: "That which will yet come, I have entrusted to Providence. I scarcely believe that a person can be more indifferent to the future than I am." *LS* 17:25 #15 and 17:208 #157 provide similar comments. In addition, the *Erziehung* (Education of the Human Race) speaks of divine power in terms of *Vorsehung* (Providence), for example in *LS* 13:434 paragraph 91.

62. The concept of silence is developed at greater length at a later point in this section.

63. See for example *LS* 13:142; 13:183–84; and 18:333 #671.

64. Selected examples: (a) Lessing's ironic description of the earlier all-encompassing role of the clergy: "Oh happy times, when the clergy was still everything in one,— thought for us and ate for us!" (LS 13:167). (b) A critique of both those who try to philosophize religion away in order to establish their own systems and those who wish to banish religion with wit, in order to amuse, can be found in *LS* 8:17. (c) An attack on clergymen who attempt to hold believers through falsehood appears in *LS* 18:245 #566.

65. See the larger statement in the *Erziehung* (Education of the Human Race), that ends with the statement, "God supposedly shows his hand in everything: only not in our errors?" (*LS* 13:415). This attitude also comes to the fore frequently in Lessing's defense of the publication of the Reimarus Fragments, for example in 13:184. A further statement in this respect:

> Does one only write in order to continually be right? I believe to have made myself just as deserving in terms of truth, when I miss it [truth], but my error is the reason why another discovers it, as when I disclose it myself. (*LS* 17:223 #173)

66. See also *LS* 13:97.

67. According to Kierkegaard, "True religiousness cannot form a party or a clique" (*JP* 4:163 #4170). See also *JP* 4:290–91 #4444; *JP* 1:420 #963; and the critique of Martin Luther in *JP* 3:727 #3724.

68. For further information concerning Kierkegaard's relationship to the Hegelian system, see James Collins, *The Mind of Kierkegaard* (Chicago: Henry Regnery Company, 1967); Naomi Lebowitz, *Kierkegaard: A Life of Allegory* (Baton Rouge and London: Louisiana State University Press, 1985); Louis Mackey, *Points of View: Readings of Kierkegaard* (Tallahassee: Florida State University Press, 1986); and Niels Thulstrup, "Kierkegaard and Hegel," *Kierkegaard and Speculative Idealism*, Niels Thulstrup and Marie Mikulová Thulstrup, eds., "Bibliotheca Kierkegaardiana" Vol. 4 (Copenhagen: C.A. Reitzels Boghandel, 1979): 52–113.

69. See also *LS* 17:203 #152, in which Lessing describes his stay in Breslau as wasted time:

I have already lost more than three years with these worthless endeavors. It is time that I get back on track again.

70. The references to this confused and depressed state of mind during the period in which Lessing occupied an official position are almost too numerous to mention. Some of the most notable include the letter from Breslau in which he exclaims:

Oh, dearest friend, your Lessing is lost! In a year you will not know him any longer. He will not know himself. Oh my time, my time, my everything, that I have—to sacrifice it in this way, for I know not what purpose! (*LS* 17:182 #132).

From Wolfenbüttel:

(a) The book dust falls more and more on my nerves, and most certainly they will soon no longer have the ability to vibrate. But that which I no longer feel, I will never forget that I once felt. I will never, because I have become dull, be unjust toward those who are not yet that way: I will despise no faculty just because I have unfortunately lost it (*LS* 17:388–89 #304).

(b) For me currently, my entire life is not infrequently so loathsome—so loathsome! I dream away my days more than I live them. Continuous work that fatigues me without giving me pleasure; an abode which, because of its complete lack of all social intercourse . . . is becoming unbearable to me; prospects of eternal, blessed monotony—all of these are things which have such a detrimental influence on my soul, and through that on my body, that I do not know whether I am ill or healthy. (*LS* 18:46 #365)

See also *LS* 18:120 #420. It would, of course, be a gross oversimplification to imply that Lessing's status as an official functionary was the sole reason for his unhappiness, particularly during the Wolfenbüttel years. However, the positions and the circumstances which they engendered are in fact the prime source of his despondency during those periods.

71. For example, in the *Dramaturgy* Lessing states:

It is permitted to everybody to have his own taste, and it is laudable to be able to give the reasons why we hold such taste. But to give to the reasons by which we justify it a character of generality, and thus make it out to be the only true taste if these be correct, means exceeding the limits permitted to the investigating amateur and instituting oneself an independent lawgiver (*HD* 51).

This viewpoint seems to form the basis for Lessing's ongoing criticism of individuals such as Gottsched, among others. In the same vein, see Lessing's criticism of a particular *Conrektor* (Deputy Headmaster) of a school in Meißen:

I know well, that it is his slightest concern to make of his subordinates rational people, if he can just make stout students of them, that is, people who blindly believe their teachers, without inquiring whether they might not be pedants (*LS* 17:25 #15).

This type of criticism is not far removed from that leveled at Goeze, who in Lessing's opinion employed the same tactics within the religious sphere.

72. In this respect, Wolfgang Kröger states in *Das Publikum als Richter: Lessing und die "kleineren Respondenten" im Fragmentenstreit* (Nendeln/Liechtenstein: KTO Press, 1979), 113, that Lessing writes, not to win the greatest possible number of adherents to a fully developed concept, but rather to induce the greatest possible number of people to enter into the process of verifying basic Christian tenets or proving them false. Ingrid Strohschneider-Kohrs expresses a similar opinion in *Vom Prinzip des Maßes in Lessings*

Kritik (Stuttgart: J. B. Metzlersche Verlagsbuchhandlung, 1969), 16.

73. In Lessing's words:

> In such conversations [with Jerusalem] there is dissension, and not seldom little or nothing is settled. But what did that matter to us? The pleasure of a hunt is always worth more than the catch. (*LS* 12:294)

74. "Set me right, if I am wrong" (*LS* 17:65 #53). A further quote:

> He has done me the honor of mentioning me three times in his little book of cut stones, and of setting me right three times. But all three times, he has either not understood me, through short-sightedness, or has not wanted to understand me, to tease me. That annoys me—. (*LS* 17:252 #198)

75. A similar sentiment is expressed in Lessing's letter from Breslau:

> Every Friday evening my heart pounds, and I do not know what I would give, if each week in the company of so many upright people I could still eat my fill, laugh my fill, and squabble my fill; especially if I could squabble my fill about things that I do not understand. (*LS* 17:180 #130)

76. In the same vein, see: (a) If I had not long since known that you are entirely too warm a friend: this letter of yours could persuade me that I have produced something unusual. But today, when you are hopefully cooler, it [the letter] would read entirely differently. And you can retract even more of it at this stage, as you read the printed piece. Here it is. You will soon find out how much the actors added to it, and how much you yourself read into it, which promoted your illusion (*LS* 18:26 #352). (b) Your critique of the inarticulate passages in my Sara became a panegyric. Your friendship allows you to detect more beauty in it than I was able to bring to it (*LS* 17:121 #79).

77. See also *LS* 17:173 #125:

> I thank you for your friendly approbation. I would thank you even more for friendly censure. For the latter could make me better, and from the former, I fear it will make me proud.

78. In this context it should be noted that Lessing's conviction as to the beneficial nature of open polemic debate extended to the point that he invited others to publicly attempt a refutation of his ideas, as can be seen for example in *LS* 17:273 #217:

> Nevertheless your written comments about my Laokoon would have been very welcome. They should still be very welcome to me in print! . . . I am entirely convinced . . . that with these reminiscences and refutations you are solely concerned with clearing up the matter, you are only concerned with truth, and not with the vanity of being a know-it-all, and putting in a few words even where one has no right to join the conversation. What do you therefore fear from me? The more faults and errors you show me, the more I will learn from you: The more I learn from you, the more grateful I will be. And this gratefulness will manifest itself in every word which I am able to retort!

A similar, highly ironic statement made in reference to Goeze:

> Goeze, someone has written to me, is ill and must go riding for two hours each day, which are exactly the two hours, which he had otherwise appointed for my refutation. If that is the case, then I will begin today to pray heartily for his recovery. (*LS* 18:296 #621)

79. See for example Lessing's impassioned statement in *LS* 10:213, as well as 18:245 #566 and 18:230 #550.

80. Literally, "rescues"—here, essays written to defend earlier authors who have been discredited or rejected by literary and religious writers.
81. See also *LS* 13:178–79.
82. See also *JP* 2:397 #1995.
83. To his father, Lessing elaborated even more completely:

> If it were possible to describe to you what sort of confusion, tribulations and labor I have been involved in this year, how discontented I have almost always been, how drained of physical and emotional vigor I have often felt: I know positively, that you would not only pardon my previous silence, but would also hold it to be the only proof of my filial esteem and love, which I have been able to give you during this time. When once I write, it is not possible for me to write other than just what I am thinking and feeling. You would have received the most unpleasant letters to read. . . . It was best, therefore, that I let [you] know nothing at all about it; which however could not happen otherwise, than if I did not write at all. (*LS* 17:239–40 #189)

See also 17:233 #181 and 18:60 #372.

A related type of silence reigned when illness and vexation with life (Verdruß) made it difficult or impossible for Lessing to involve himself in any sort of literary expression. For example: (a) A vexing life, when one is up and about and vegetates, and is thought to be healthy, without so being! Before my illness, I was on a roll with my work, as I seldom have been before. I still cannot get back into it, no matter how I set about it (*LS* 17:213 #160). (b) From my silence you can infer how I am doing. Worse than a year ago. These lines, for which I must apply force to myself to even manage to scribble them down, are, in the strictest truth the first in six weeks. I can do nothing, even if my life should depend on it (*LS* 18:49 #366).
In this context, refer also to *LS* 17:62 #52 and 18:94 #399.

84. In the same vein, see the reference to his father's death (*LS* 17:391–92 #306) in which Lessing declares his intention to honor the memory of the deceased by paying the debts left at his death. Upon the death of his mother, Lessing states that the best way to show his sorrow is through remembrance of and financial help to the sister who cared for her in her waning years (*LS* 18:225 #545).
85. This controlled expression of feeling finds a metaphorical presentation in *LS* 17:384 #301:

> How reluctantly I decline the pleasure of taking the waters in your company! To defer it for so long, however, is in no way prudent, neither for the fountain, nor for the one whom it should help.

See also *LS* 18:57 #371; 17:402 #315; and 17:418 #327.
86. Lessing married Eva König fairly late in his life.
87. Lessing very clearly speaks by remaining silent when he writes:

> my wife is dead. If you had known her!—But they say it is nothing but self-praise to extol one's wife. Fine, then I will say nothing further about her. But if you had known her! (*LS* 18:262 #589)

In the same sense, the difficulty of this loss, and the emotional trauma involved in it come to clear expression in the restrained simplicity of these words:

> My wife is dead: and I have now gained this experience as well. I am happy that there cannot be too many such experiences still left for me to have; and I am at peace. (*LS* 18:262 #588)

88. See, for example, the letter to Johann Wilhelm Gleim in which Lessing writes concerning patriotism:

> I have absolutely . . . no concept of love for the fatherland, and it seems to me in
> the highest degree to be a heroic weakness, which I very gladly dispense with.—
> But allow me to write nothing further concerning this. (*LS* 17:158 #110)

89. An example of the need to protect the opportunity to have one's work performed
appears in *LS* 18:293 #617:

> My piece has nothing to do with our current parsons; and I do not wish to per-
> sonally bungle the possibility of its finally getting into the theater, even if it
> should only be in a hundred years.

90. Lessing's style of writing will be discussed in greater detail at a later point.
An example of Lessing's polemic reluctance to multiply words can be found in *LS*
13:43:

> Now let us examine more closely the statements which are supposedly so clear
> and correct.—I shudder at having to use a multitude of unnecessary words.

Wolfgang Kröger explores this phenomenon of polemical silence in *Publikum*, 39–51.
Emil Staiger in "Lessings Prosa: Eine Vorlesung," *Dichtung und Deutung: Gedächtnisschrift für Hans M. Wolff*, Karl S. Guthke, Hsg. (Bern: A. Francke Verlag, 1961),
148 touches upon this point in conjunction with Lessing's conversational form of presentation when he states:

> In conversation one ventures to say many things, which in a lecture hall he
> would prefer to weigh once again. Therefore, when Lessing, even as an author,
> chooses the dialogue, the form of heated debate, certainly his aversion to all
> positivity, to all that is dogmatically fixed has a share in that. It would be false
> to name this cowardice. Lessing was never lacking in valor. It is rather respect
> for the ambiguity of vigorous life that moves him to such an action.

91. Lessing states further:

> No one enjoys subjecting himself to labors from which he receives absolutely
> no benefit, neither money, nor honor, nor pleasure. In the time which a play
> ten sheets long costs me, I could well and gladly, with less effort, write a hun-
> dred other sheets. . . . Why should I for nothing, and again for nothing, put my-
> self to the rack for six weeks? . . . every artist has his price; every artist
> attempts to live as comfortably as possible from his work: why not the poet as
> well? . . . Very well, cash for the fish————. . . . Money is exactly that which I
> lack. (*LS* 18:67–68 #375)

For similar statements see also *LS* 17:257 #202; 18:309 #637; 18:285 #611;
18:120–21 #420; 18:81 #387.

92. See *LS* 18:287 #613 and 18:289 #615.

93. Lessing's words:

> A discerning author, it seems to me, establishes his methods best in accordance
> with this little saying. He should first seek out someone with whom he can dis-
> pute: in this way he will come little by little into the subject matter, and the rest
> will take care of itself. (*LS* 10:84)

An illustration of this method of procedure can also be seen in Lessing's entrance into
the debate with Klotz:

> I had waited a long time to see if anyone desired to tackle the crude Goliath of
> the learned Philistines: finally I could not possibly endure his idiotic derision
> any longer, without throwing a couple of stones from my pocket at his head.
> (*LS* 17:284 #226)

Excellent examples are also found in Lessing's statements concerning his publication of the Reimarus Fragments in *LS* 13:208; 13:184; and 13:142.

Of *Laokoon* Lessing writes:

> To oppose this false taste, and to counteract these unfounded opinions, is the principal object of the following observations.
>
> They have arisen casually, and have grown to their present size rather in consequence of the course of my reading than through any methodical development of general principles. They are rather irregular *collectanea* for a book, than a book. Yet, I flatter myself that, even as such, they will not be wholly despised. We Germans have no lack of systematic treatises. (*L* 57)

See also *LS* 9:7.

94. Horst Steinmetz, in "Kritiker," observes that, although it is fairly simple to isolate the many contradictions in the *Hamburg Dramaturgy*, these have little more than statistical meaning. In his opinion, it is of far greater interest to determine why someone as shrewd as Lessing should exhibit such contradiction in his work. Using the example of Lessing's innovative differentiation between *Furcht* (fear) and *Schrecken* (terror) in traditional tragedy, Steinmetz concludes that Lessing's new definition arose, not as an attempt to reinterpret Aristotle, but rather through "the accidental necessity of providing security for his own critique of [Christian Felix] Weiß's drama" (34–35).

Steinmetz goes on to point out that this does not mean that Lessing came to his results in a purely *ad hoc* manner as the result of accidental external stimulus, nor that he had never thought of this definition in these terms before. Rather:

> For us, the issue is to recognize in what an adroit manner Lessing knows how to bring his findings into play at the right moment; that he only brings them into play when it seems necessary to him, indeed where he is literally forced to do so. (Ibid., 35)

Dan L. Flory agrees in "Lessing, Mendelssohn and Der nordische Aufseher: A Study in Lessing's Critical Procedure," *Lessing Yearbook 7* (München: Max Hueber Verlag, 1975): 142, that "Lessing argued not necessarily on the basis of pre-established criteria but according to his current goal," a fact which often produced an "apparent shift of values."

95. See a similar statement in *LS* 8:14: "One does not despise a tree because of its unsightly blossoms, if it is to be valued because of its fruit."

96. Staiger, "Lessings Prosa," 150–51.

97. In reference to the question of communication, Frederick Sontag observes in *A Kierkegaard Handbook* (Atlanta: John Knox Press, 1979), 60:

> The problem is to find a way to communicate inwardness in a manner that will not be treated outwardly and thus become distorted. Little is possible by way of direct communication, for what is inward can never be conveyed as such. Yet the translation into indirect modes also places a religious message in danger of being misunderstood. There is no safe medium to which we can turn for communication in a manner safe from distortion.

98. Lars Bejerholm, "Communication," *Concepts and Alternatives in Kierkegaard*, Marie Mikulová Thulstrup, ed., "Bibliotheca Kierkegaardiana," Vol. 3 (Copenhagen: C. A. Reitzels Boghandel, 1980), 56.

99. See Theresa A. Sandok, "Kierkegaard on Irony and Humor," Ph. D dissertation, Notre Dame, 1975, 65.

100. Lee M. Capel, "Historical Introduction," *The Concept of Irony* by Søren Kierkegaard [1965] (Bloomington: Indiana University Press, 1968), 37.

101. Lessing's words: "I will guide myself, rather, back into my path, if a stroller even has a path" (*LS* 9: 120).

102. Mummenhoff, "Darstellungsweise," 17. The reader is referred to the bibliography at the end of this study for a listing of many in-depth analyses of Lessing's style of writing. They are too numerous to be individually mentioned here.

103. Gotthold Ephraim Lessing, *Laocoon*, trans. Rt. Hon. Sir Robert Phillimore, Bart. (London: George Routledge & Sons, Ltd., no date [1874]), 60:

> I confess that the unfavourable side glance which he casts upon Virgil startled me at first, and in the next place the comparison with Philoctetes. From this I will take my point of departure, and write down my thoughts in the order in which they have been developed.

104. See also Lessing's process of thinking aloud in *LS* 12:45–46.

105. Staiger, "Lessings Prosa," 146.

106. See also *LS* 12:102 for a similar admission, as well as 8:93. Numerous examples of this honesty appear in Lessing's private letters as well. For example: 17:398–99 #313; 18:220 #539; 18:101 #404; and 17:78–79 #57.

107. Also of interest in this context is Lessing's monologue concerning unanswered letters in *LS* 17:190 #141.

108. See also the lively description in *LS* 13:56 ff., esp. 64, of Goeze's depiction of Mary Magdalene which, as Lessing insists, transforms her into the harlequin of the gospel harmony. An analysis of Lessing's uses of ironic wit and his polemic style would demand an entire work in and of itself. For individual discussions in this respect, see, among others: Norbert W. Feinäugle, "Lessings Streitschriften: Überlegungen zu Wesen und Methode der literarischen Polemik," *Lessing Yearbook 1* (München: Max Hueber Verlag, 1969): 126–49; Klaus Lazarowicz, *Verkehrte Welt: Vorstudien zu einer Geschichte der deutschen Satire* (Tübingen: Max Niemeyer Verlag, 1963); and Marion Gräfin Hoensbroech, *Die List der Kritik: Lessings kritische Schriften und Dramen* (München: Wilhelm Fink Verlag, 1976).

109. Mummenhoff, "Darstellungsweise," 15. Volker Nölle's observations, presented in *Subjektivität*, 233–34, are enlightening on this point. Nölle states that the relative lack of sharpness and clarity inherent in the usage of metaphor is a matter of conscious design, because the imagery is able to express in a covert manner that which would have been overly daring as a direct statement. In this sense, the metaphors both disguise and disclose that which is actually intended. As he continues:

> These metaphors only apparently elucidate that which earlier had already been said: in reality, however, they at the same time "skip over" a series of elements which, in objective argumentation, would have to be precisely demonstrated. This shifting of meaning is executed inconspicuously, with laconic matter-of-factness. The transfer of emphasis strides along with the summons of the reader to a spontaneous opinion. Thanks to the management which brings the metaphors into play in such a superior manner, clarity and unequivocalness are suggested, and all problems appear to be eliminated; but this clarity and unequivocalness are only fictitious, corresponding to the fictitiousness of the metaphors.

110. Another short example, written to criticize the poor quality of Greek translations in Germany: "Unsere witzige Köpfe sind meistens schlechte Griechen, und unsere guten Griechen sind meistens— —" ("Our clever thinkers are mostly wretched Greeks, and our good Greeks are mostly— —") (*LS* 17:210 #158). See also: *LS* 17:314 #253; 17:170–71 #122; 18:48–49 #365; and 13:87.

111. A second example, drawn from the *Duplik* (Defendant's Rejoinder):

Das glaubte ich; das glaub ich noch.—War ich aber, bin ich aber darum völlig des Ungennanten Meinung? Wollte ich darum, will ich darum eben dahinaus, wo er hinauswollte?

Mit nichten!—Ich gab den Vordersatz zu; und leugnete die Folge. (*LS* 13:25)

I believed that; I believe it still.—But was I, am I because of that, entirely of the same opinion as the anonymous man? Because of that, did I wish, do I wish to get at precisely that which he was driving at?

By no means!—I conceded the premise; and disavowed the result.

112. Staiger, "Lessings Prosa," 147.
113. Jens, "Feldzüge," 52–53. Klaus Lazarowicz states in *Verkehrte Welt*, 169:

These are accusing questions, which Lessing strings together here in carefully calculated intensification; the questions of a passionately excited man, who certainly knows how to control his emotions and understands how to recoin them as sarcasm and cynicism. . . .Here the orator wielded the feather of the author Lessing. And the art of the author consists, above all, in the fact that he is able to realize with apparent ease the intentions of the orator.

114. Similarly, Lessing ironically excuses Dusch:

To be sure, Mr. Dusch certainly did not wish to say that, but rather, his pen, once having been lifted, wrote it down against his will. (*LS* 8:98)

More than once, Lessing recorded the confusion of his contemporaries concerning his personal standpoint. See for example *LS* 17:96 #61 and 18:244 #565.
115. Jürgen Schröder, in *Gotthold Ephraim Lessing: Sprache und Drama* (München: Wilhelm Fink Verlag, 1972), 21, expresses much the same thought when he writes:

[Lessing] prefers to invent . . . his partners, and even where he allows them to take the floor in their own name, they remain a shadowy vis-a-vis, which he has molded according to his own plan.

Dan Flory seems likewise to touch on this idea when he speaks of the (not necessarily intentional) distortion of Lessing's polemic opponents in "Lessing," esp. 141–42.
116. Note that Lessing also speaks of assuming a pose or posture (Positur) in his theological debate, as a tactical measure. See *LS* 18:265 #594.

Chapter 3. The Significance of Lessing's Pseudonymity in the Overall Complex of the Pseudonyms

1. S. H. Butcher, *Aristotle's Theory of Poetry and Fine Art* (New York: Dover Publications, Inc., 1951), 35.
2. For a further analysis of the relationship between drama and history in Lessing's thought, see Alan Menhennet, "Historical and Dramatic Truth in Lessing," *Lessing Yearbook 19* (Detroit: Wayne State University Press, 1988).
3. Roberts, *Faith, Reason, and History*, 135.
4. Taylor, *Pseudonymous Authorship*, 81, 84.
5. Georg Lukács, "The Foundering of Form against Life: Søren Kierkegaard and Regine Olsen," *Søren Kierkegaard*, ed. Harold Bloom, (New York: Chelsea House Publishers, 1989), 6.
6. Lewis White Beck, *Early German Philosophy* (Cambridge, Mass.: The Belknap

Press, 1969), 341–42.

7. Hans Urs von Balthasar, *Prometheus: Studien zur Geschichte des deutschen Idealismus* (Heidelberg: F. H. Kerle Verlag, 1947), 45.

8. Gordon E. Michalson, Jr., "Kierkegaard's Debt to Lessing: Response to Whisenant," *Modern Theology* 6.4 (July 1990): 382.

9. See, for example, *JP* 1:53–54 #131 and *JP* 2:81 #1288. Concerning Kierkegaard's productivity in relationship to himself, see among others *JP* 6:481 #6843.

10. Cappelørn, "Retrospective," 25–26. For Kierkegaard's own report on the difficulties he experienced in describing the events of his life, see *JP* 6:481 #6843.

11. See, for example, Kierkegaard's personal statement and protestation to this effect, which forms the whole of the *Point of View*. Niels Cappelørn presents an instructive analysis of this assertion by Kierkegaard in his article "Kierkegaards eigener 'Gesichtspunkt' 'Vorwärts zu leben, aber rückwärts zu verstehen'," *Neue Zeitschrift für systematische Theologie und Religionsphilosophie* 17 (1975): 61–75.

12. As early as 1843, the year in which *Either/Or* appeared, Kierkegaard was able to formulate in his journal the vision of his task as an author which would guide him throughout the entirety of his production, as can be seen in *JP* 5:226 #5646.

13. Most recently, see Sylviane Agacinski, "On a Thesis," *Søren Kierkegaard*, ed. Harold Bloom, (New York: Chelsea House Publishers, 1989), 118–19; T. F. Morris, "Kierkegaard's Understanding of Socrates," *International Journal for Philosophy of Religion* 19.1–2 (1986): 105–11; and Harold Sarf, "Reflections on Kierkegaard's Socrates," *Journal of the History of Ideas* 44.2 (April-June 1983): 255–76.

14. See Louis Jacobs, "The Problem of the *Akedah* in Jewish Thought," *Kierkegaard's "Fear and Trembling": Critical Appraisals*, ed. Robert L. Perkins, (University: The University of Alabama Press, 1981), 1–9; and Ronald M. Green, "Abraham, Isaac, and the Jewish Tradition: An Ethical Reappraisal," *The Journal of Religious Ethics* 10.1 (Spring 1982): 1–21.

15. R. Z. Friedman, "Looking for Abraham: Kierkegaard and the Knight of Anxiety," *International Philosophical Quarterly* 27.3 (September 1987): 252.

16. Ibid., 260.

17. Ibid., 262.

18. George Pattison, "A Drama of Love and Death: Michael Pedersen Kierkegaard and Regine Olsen Revisited," *History of European Ideas* 12.1 (1990): 90. In this respect, see also Georg Lukács, "The Foundering of Form against Life: Søren Kierkegaard and Regine Olsen," *Søren Kierkegaard,* ed. Harold Bloom (New York and Philadelphia: Chelsea House Publishers, 1989).

19. Schlegel, *Ausgabe*, 2: 112.

20. Jean-François Marquet, "Le Message et son Labyrinthe," *Critique* 222 (novembre 1965): 951.

21. Thompson, *Kierkegaard*, 187.

22. Ibid., 153.

23. See Chapter 1, note 20.

Bibliography

Primary Sources

Butcher, S. H. *Aristotle's Theory of Poetry and Fine Art.* New York: Dover Publications, Inc., 1951.

Kierkegaard, Søren. *The Concept of Anxiety.* Translated by Reidar Thomte. Princeton: Princeton University Press, 1980.

————. *The Concept of Dread.* Translated by Walter Lowrie. 1944. Reprint. Princeton: Princeton University Press, 1967.

————. *The Concept of Irony.* Translated by Lee M. Capel. 1965. Reprint. Bloomington: Indiana University Press, 1968.

————. *Concluding Unscientific Postscript.* Translated by David F. Swenson. 1941. Reprint. Princeton: Princeton University Press, 1968.

————. *Either/Or.* Translated by David F. Swenson and Lillian Marvin Swenson. 2 vols. 1944. Reprint. Princeton: Princeton University Press, 1971.

————. *Fear and Trembling and The Sickness unto Death.* Translated by Walter Lowrie. 1941. Reprint. Princeton: Princeton University Press, 1968.

————. *Fear and Trembling/Repetition.* Translated by Howard V. Hong and Edna H. Hong. Princeton: Princeton University Press, 1983.

————. *Letters and Documents.* Translated by Henrik Rosenmeier. Princeton: Princeton University Press, 1978.

————. *Philosophical Fragments.* Translated by David F. Swenson and Howard V. Hong. 1936. Reprint. Princeton: Princeton University Press, 1967.

————. *Philosophical Fragments/ Johannes Climacus.* Translated by Howard V. Hong and Edna H. Hong. Princeton: Princeton University Press, 1985.

————. *The Point of View for my Work as an Author.* Translated by Walter Lowrie. New York: Harper Torchbooks–Harper and Row, Publishers, 1962.

————. *Repetition.* Translated by Walter Lowrie. Princeton: Princeton University Press, 1946.

————. *The Sickness unto Death.* Translated by Howard V. Hong and Edna H. Hong. Princeton: Princeton University Press, 1980.

————. *Søren Kierkegaard's Journals and Papers.* Edited and translated by Howard V. Hong and Edna H. Hong. 7 vols. Bloomington: Indiana University Press, 1975.

————. *Søren Kierkegaards Papirer*. Udg. P. A. Heiberg og V. Kuhr. 20 binder. København (Copenhagen): Gyldendalske Boghandel Nordisk Forlag, 1909.

————. *Søren Kierkegaards Samlede Vaerker*. Udg. A. B. Drachmann, J. L. Heiberg og H. D. Lange. Anden Udgave. 15 binder. Kjøbenhavn (Copenhagen): Gyldendalske Boghandel, Nordisk Forlag, 1920.

————. *Stages on Life's Way*. Translated by Walter Lowrie. Princeton: Princeton University Press, 1945.

Lessing, Gotthold Ephraim. *Gotthold Ephraim Lessings sämtliche Schriften*. Hsg. Karl Lachmann und Franz Muncker. 3. Aufl. 23 Bände. Leipzig: G. J. Göschen'sche Verlagshandlung, 1904.

————. *Lessings Werke*. Hsg. Franz Muncker. 12 Bände. Stuttgart, 1890.

————. *Lessings Werke*. Hsg. Waldemar Oehlke und Eduard Stemplinger. Lebensbild von Julius Petersen. Leipzig: Deutsches Verlagshaus Bong und Co., n. d.

————. *Hamburg Dramaturgy*. Translated by Helen Zimmern. New York: Dover Publications, Inc., 1962.

————. *Laocoon*. Translated by Rt. Hon. Sir Robert Phillimore, Bart. London: George Routledge and Sons, Ltd., [1874].

Poole, Roger and Henrik Stangerup, eds. *The Laughter is on My Side: An Imaginative Introduction to Kierkegaard*. Princeton: Princeton University Press, 1989.

Secondary Works

LESSING AND KIERKEGAARD

von Borman, Claus. "Kierkegaard und Lessing." *Kierkegaard und die deutsche Philosophie seiner Zeit*. Hsg. Heinrich Anz, Peter Kemp, und Friedrich Schmöe. München: Wilhelm Fink Verlag, 1980.

Campbell, Richard. "Lessing's Problem and Kierkegaard's Answer." *Scottish Journal of Theology* (Edinburgh) 19.1 (1966): 35–54.

Colette, Jacques. "Kierkegaard et Lessing." *Revue des Sciences Philosophiques et Théologiques* 44 (1960): 3–39.

Gerlach, Hans-Martin. "Wahrheit und Geschichte/Lessing oder Kierkegaard?" *Lessing-Konferenz, Halle 1979*. Hsg. Hans-Georg Werner. Teil 2. Halle (Saale): Martin-Luther-Universität Wissenschaftliche Beiträge, 1980.

Lunding, Erik. "Lessing und Kierkegaard." *Orbis Litterarum* 2 (1944): 158–87.

Michalson, G. E. Jr. "Kierkegaard's Debt to Lessing: Response to Whisenant." *Modern Theology* 6.4 (July 1990): 379–84.

————. "Lessing, Kierkegaard and the 'Ugly Ditch': a Reexamination." *Journal of Religion* 59.3 (1979): 324–34.

————. *Lessing's "Ugly Ditch": A Study of Theology and History*. University Park and London: The Pennsylvania State University Press, 1985.

Requadt, Paul. "Lessing, Schlegel, Kierkegaard." *Neue Schweizer Rundschau* 36/37 (1929): 103–8.

Whisenant, James. "Kierkegaard's Use of Lessing." *Modern Theology* 6.3 (April 1990): 259–72.

LESSING

Albrecht, Wolfgang. "Lessing-Forschung 1984 bis 1988." *Weimarer Beiträge: Zeitschrift für Literaturwissenschaft, Ästhetik und Kulturtheorie* 36.7 (1990): 1164–80.

Allison, Henry E. *Lessing and the Enlightenment: His Philosophy of Religion and its Relation to XVIII Century Thought.* Ann Arbor: The University of Michigan Press, 1966.

Althaus, Thomas. *Das Uneigentliche ist das Eigentliche: Metaphorische Darstellung in der Prosa bei Lessing und Lichtenberg.* Münster: Aschendorff, 1991.

Arnold, Heinz L. "Dokumente zum Streit." *Text + Kritik: Zeitschrift für Literatur.* 26/27 (1970): 53–65.

Bahr, Ehrhard, Edward P. Harris, und Laurence G. Lyon, Hsg. *Humanität und Dialog.* Detroit: Wayne State University Press, 1982.

von Balthasar, Hans Urs. *Prometheus: Studien zur Geschichte des deutschen Idealismus.* Heidelberg: F. H. Kerle Verlag, 1947.

Barner, Wilfried, Gunter Grimm, Helmuth Kiesel, and Martin Kramer. *Lessing: Epoche—Werk—Wirkung.* München: C. H. Beck'sche Verlagsbuchhandlung, 1975.

Barnett, Stuart. "'Über die Grenzen': Semiotics and Subjectivity in Lessing's *Hamburgische Dramaturgie.*" *The German Quarterly* 60.3 (Summer 1987): 407–19.

Barth, Karl. *Protestant Thought: From Rousseau to Ritschl.* Translated by Brian Cozens and H. H. Hartwell. New York: Harper and Row, 1959.

Batley, Edward M. *Catalyst of Enlightenment: Gotthold Ephraim Lessing.* Bern: Peter Lang, 1990.

Bauer, Gerhard und Sibylle Bauer, Hsg. *Gotthold Ephraim Lessing.* Darmstadt: Wissenschaftliche Buchgesellschaft, 1968.

Beck, Lewis White. *Early German Philosophy.* Cambridge, Mass.: The Belknap Press, 1969.

Bender, Wolfgang. "Rhetorische Tradition bei Lessing." *Lessing Yearbook 21.* Detroit: Wayne State University Press, 1990.

Bennett, Benjamin. "Reason, Error and the Shape of History: Lessing's Nathan and Lessing's God." *Lessing Yearbook 9.* München: Max Hueber Verlag, 1977.

Berger, Arnold E. *Lessings geistesgeschichtliche Stellung.* Leipzig: Ernst Hofmann und Co., 1929.

von Biederman, Flodoard Freiherr. *Gotthold Ephraim Lessings Gespräche nebst sonstigen Zeugnissen aus seinem Umgang.* Berlin: Propyläen Verlag, 1924.

Bohm, Arnd. "Gottsched's *Sterbender Cato* as a Pretext for Lessing's *Emilia Galotti.*" *Seminar: A Journal of Germanic Studies* 24.1 (February 1988): 1–19.

Bohnen, Klaus. *Geist und Buchstabe. Zum Prinzip des kritischen Verfahrens in Lessings literarästhetischen und theologischen Schriften.* Köln: Böhlau Verlag, 1974.

Brandl, Benedict. *Lessings Fragmenten-Streit.* Pilsen: Maasch, 1908.

Braun, Julius W. *Lessing im Urteile seiner Zeitgenossen.* Berlin, 1884.

Briegleb, Klaus. *Lessings Anfänge 1742–1746. Zur Grundlegung kritischer Sprachdemokratie.* Frankfurt: Athenäum Verlag, 1971.

Brown, F. Andrew. *Gotthold Ephraim Lessing.* New York: Twayne Publishers Inc., 1971.

Burgard, Peter J. "Dialogue and the community of writing." *Studies on Voltaire and the Eighteenth Century* 264 (1989): 1178–82.

Cassirer, Ernst. "Die Idee der Religion bei Lessing und Mendelssohn." *Bulletin des Leo Baeck Instituts* 84 (1989): 5–22.

Corngold, Stanley. "Wit and Judgment in the Eighteenth Century: Lessing and Kant." *MLN* 102.3 (April 1987): 461–82.

Danzel, Th. W. und G. E. Guhrauer. *G. E. Lessing, sein Leben und seine Werke.* Hsg. W. von Maltzahn und R. Boxberger. 1850. Reprint. Berlin, 1880–81.

Daunicht, Richard. *Lessing im Gespräch: Berichte und Urteile von Freunden und Zeitgenossen.* München: Wilhelm Fink Verlag, 1971.

Demetz, Peter. "Die Folgenlosigkeit Lessings." *Merkur* 25 (1971): 727–41.

Dilthey, Wilhelm. *Das Erlebnis und die Dichtung.* 1905. Reprint. Göttingen: Vandenhoeck und Ruprecht, 1970.

Drews, Wolfgang. *Gotthold Ephraim Lessing in Selbstzeugnissen und Bilddokumenten.* Hamburg: Rowohlt, 1962.

Dvoretzky, Edward, Hsg. *Lessing. Dokumente zur Wirkungsgeschichte 1755–1968.* Göppingen: Verlag Alfred Kümmerle, 1971.

Feinäugle, Norbert W. "Lessings Streitschriften: Überlegungen zu Wesen und Methode der literarischen Polemik." *Lessing Yearbook 1.* München: Max Hueber Verlag, 1969.

Flake, Otto. *Die Verurteilung des Sokrates: Biographische Essays aus 6 Jahrzehnten.* Hsg. Fredy Gröbli-Schaub und Rolf Hochhuth. Heidelberg: Verlag Lambert Schneider, 1970.

Flory, Dan L. "Lessing, Mendelssohn and Der nordische Aufseher: A Study in Lessing's Critical Procedure." *Lessing Yearbook 7.* München: Max Hueber Verlag, 1975.

Friedrich, Wolf-Hartmut. "Sophokles, Aristoteles und Lessing." *Euphorion* 57 (1963): 4–27.

Garland, H. B. *Lessing: The Founder of Modern German Literature.* London: McMillan and Co., 1962.

Göpfert, Herbert G., Hsg. *Das Bild Lessings in der Geschichte.* Heidelberg: Verlag Lambert Schneider, 1981.

Grimm, Gunter E. "'Ich sehne mich herzlich wieder nach Deutschland'—Lessings Italienreise von 1775." *Lessing Yearbook 17.* Detroit: Wayne State University Press, 1986.

Guidry, Glenn A. "A Communication Model in Lessing's Dramas?" *Postscript* 5 (1988): 55–60.

———. "Dialogue and Utopia in Lessing." *Monatshefte* 80.2 (1988): 149–61.

Guthke, Karl S. "Der Glückspieler als Autor: Überlegungen zur 'Gestalt' Lessings im Sinne der inneren Biographie." *Euphorion: Zeitschrift für Literaturgeschichte.* 71 (1977): 353–82.

———. "Der Philosoph im Spielkasino: Das Bild der Persönlichkeit Lessings in neuerer Sicht." *Schweizer Monatshefte für Politik, Wirtschaft, Kultur* 59 (1979): 697–712.

———. *Der Stand der Lessing-Forschung 1932–62.* Stuttgart: J. B. Metzlersche Verlagsbuchhandlung, 1965.

——— und Heinrich Schneider. *Gotthold Ephraim Lessing.* Stuttgart: J. B. Metzlersche Verlagsbuchhandlung, 1967.

————. "Grundlagen der Lessingforschung: Neuere Ergebnisse, Probleme, Aufgaben." *Wolfenbütteler Studien zur Aufklärung* 2 (1975): 10–46.

————. "Lessing-Literatur 1963–1968." *Lessing Yearbook 1*. München: Max Hueber Verlag, 1969.

Harris, Edward P. und Richard E. Schade, Hsg. *Lessing in heutiger Sicht*. Bremen: Jacobi Verlag, 1977.

Heitner, Robert R. "Rationalism and Irrationalism in Lessing." *Lessing Yearbook 5*. München: Max Hueber Verlag, 1973.

Heller, Agnes. "Aufklärung gegen Fundamentalismus: Der Fall Lessing." *Lessing Yearbook 19*. Detroit: Wayne State University Press, 1988.

Heller, Peter. *Dialectics and Nihilism: Essays on Lessing, Nietzsche, Mann and Kafka*. Amherst: The University of Massachusetts Press, 1966.

————. "Lessing's Historical Dialectic." *Lessing Yearbook 13*. München: Max Hueber Verlag, 1981.

————. "Zum Thema der Misanthropie bei Lessing." *Euphorion* 68 (1974): 110–12.

Hibberd, John L., und H. B. Nisbet, Hsg. *Texte, Motive und Gestalten der Goethezeit*. Tübingen: Max Niemeyer Verlag, 1989.

Hildebrandt, Dieter. *Lessing: Biographie einer Emanzipation*. München: Hanser Verlag, 1979.

Hill, David. "Lessing: die Sprache der Toleranz." *Deutsche Vierteljahrsschrift für Literaturwissenschaft und Geistesgeschichte* 64.2 (Juni 1990): 218–46.

Hillen, Gerd. *Lessing Chronik: Daten zu Leben und Werk*. München: Carl Hanser Verlag, 1979.

Hoensbroech, Marion Gräfin. *Die List der Kritik: Lessings kritische Schriften und Dramen*. München: Wilhelm Fink Verlag, 1976.

Höhle, Thomas. "Friedrich Schlegels Auseinandersetzung mit Lessing: Zum Problem des Verhältnisses zwischen Romantik und Aufklärung." *Weimarer Beiträge* 23 (1977): 121–35.

Hüskens-Hasselbeck, Karin. *Stil und Kritik*. München: Wilhelm Fink Verlag, 1978.

Immisch, Otto. "Beiträge zur Beurteilung der stilistischen Kunst in Lessings Prosa, insonderheit der Streitschriften." *Text + Kritik: Zeitschrift für Literatur* 26/27 (1970): 26–38.

Jacobs, Jürgen. *Lessing*. München und Zürich: Artemis Verlag, 1986.

Jahn, Günter. "'Gedanken unter der Feder reif werden lassen'—Anregungen aus Lessings Schreibwerkstatt." *Der Deutschunterricht* 41.3 (June 1989): 51–64.

Janson, Deborah. "The Emancipation which Enslaved." *New German Review* 1 (1985): 15–27.

Jens, Walter. *Von deutscher Rede*. München: R. Piper und Co. Verlag, 1969.

Keller, Ernst. *Kritische Intelligenz, G. E. Lessing, F. Schlegel, L. Borne*. Bern: Herbert Lang, 1976.

Knodt, Eva M. *"Negative Philosophie" und dialogische Kritik*. Tübingen: Max Niemeyer Verlag, 1988.

Koch, Franz. "Lessing und der Irrationalismus." *Deutsche Vierteljahrsschrift für Literaturwissenschaft und Geistesgeschichte* 6 (1928): 114–43.

von König, Dominik. *Natürlichkeit und Wirklichkeit: Studien zu Lessings "Nathan der Weise"*. Bonn: Bouvier Verlag Herbert Grundmann, 1976.

Korff, Hermann August. *Lessing. Kleist. Schiller: Drei Vorträge*. Leipzig: Koehler und Amelang, 1961.

Körner, Josef. *Bibliographisches Handbuch des deutschen Schrifttums*. Bern: A. Francke Verlag, 1966.

Köster, Albert. "Lessing und Gottsched." *Euphorion* 1 (1894): 64–71.

Kröger, Wolfgang. *Das Publikum als Richter: Lessing und die "kleineren Respondenten" im Fragmentenstreit*. Nendeln/Liechtenstein: KTO Press, 1979.

Kuhles, Doris. "'Er verlangt, ihm nachzudenken.' Zum neuen Band der Weimarer Lessing-Bibliographie." *Lessing Yearbook 21*. Detroit: Wayne State University Press, 1990.

———. *Lessing-Bibliographie 1971–1985*. Berlin und Weimar: Aufbau-Verlag, 1988.

Lamport, F. J. *Lessing and the Drama*. Oxford: Clarendon Press, 1981.

Lazarowicz, Klaus. *Verkehrte Welt: Vorstudien zu einer Geschichte der deutschen Satire*. Tübingen: Max Niemeyer Verlag, 1963.

Leisegang, Hans. *Lessings Weltanschauung*. Leipzig: Felix Meiner Verlag, 1931.

Lützeler, Paul Michael. "Die marxistische Lessing-Rezeption: Darstellung und Kritik am Beispiel von Mehring und Lukács." *Lessing Yearbook 3*. München: Max Hueber Verlag, 1971.

Mann, Otto und Rotraut Straube-Mann. *Lessing-Kommentar*. München: Winkler Verlag, 1971.

———. *Lessing: Sein und Leistung*. Berlin: Walter de Gruyter und Co., 1961.

———. "Problem und Problematik des Lessing-Bildes in der Philosophie und Literaturwissenschaft." *Boletin de Estudios Germanicos* 8 (1970): 69–80.

Martinson, Steven D. "The Cunning of Deceit in Lessing's Major Works." *Lessing Yearbook 14*. München: Max Hueber Verlag, 1982.

Maurer, Warren R. "The Naturalist Image of Lessing." *Germanic Review* 44 (1969): 31–44.

Mayer, Hans. *Lessing und die Zeit der Aufklärung*. Göttingen: Vandenhoeck und Ruprecht, 1968.

———. "Lessing und Aristoteles." *Festschrift für Bernhard Blume*. Hsg. Egon Schwarz, Hunter G. Hannum und Edgar Lohner. Göttingen: Vandenhoeck und Ruprecht, 1967.

Mehring, Franz. *Die Lessing-Legende: Zur Geschichte und Kritik des preußischen Despotismus und der klassischen Literatur*. 1893. Reprint. Berlin: Ullstein, 1972.

Menhennet, Alan. "Historical and Dramatic Truth in Lessing." *Lessing Yearbook 19*. Detroit: Wayne State University Press, 1988.

Metzger, Willi. *Die Entwicklung von Lessings Briefstil: Eine Analyse der gestaltbildenden seelischen Verfassungen*. Gießen: Wilhelm Schmitz Verlag, 1927.

Meyer, Jochen. "Kommentierte Auswahl-Bibliographie." *Text + Kritik: Zeitschrift für Literatur* 26/27 (1970): 66–75.

Michelsen, Peter. "Der Kritiker des Details: Lessing in den 'Briefen die Neueste Literatur betreffend'." *Wolfenbütteler Studien zur Aufklärung* 2 (1975): 148–81.

———. *Der unruhige Bürger*. Würzburg: Königshausen und Neumann, 1990.

Milde, Wolfgang. "Textkritische Anmerkungen zu drei Lessingbriefen. Zur Zuverlässigkeit der Textwiedergabe." *Lessing Yearbook 17*. Detroit: Wayne State University Press, 1986.

Morton, Michael. "*Verum est factum*: Critical Realism and the Discourse of Autonomy." *The German Quarterly* 64.2 (1991): 149–65.

Mummenhoff, Wilhelm. "Die Darstellungsweise Lessings in seinen prosaischen Schriften." *73. Jahresbericht des Gymnasiums zu Recklinghausen Schuljahr 1902–1903*. Recklinghausen: J. Bauer, 1903.

Neumann, Peter Horst. *Der Preis der Mündigkeit: Über Lessings Dramen*. Stuttgart: Klett-Cotta, 1977.

Nisbet, H. B. "Lessing and the Search for Truth." *Publications of the English Goethe Society* 43 (1972/73): 72–95.

Nölle, Volker. *Subjektivität und Wirklichkeit in Lessings dramatischem und theologischem Werk*. Berlin: Erich Schmidt Verlag, 1977.

Nolting, Winfried. *Die Dialektik der Empfindung*. Stuttgart: Franz Steiner Verlag Wiesbaden GmbH, 1986.

Oehlke, Waldemar. *Lessing und seine Zeit*. 2 Bände. München: C. H. Beck'sche Verlagsbuchhandlung, 1919.

O'Flaherty, James C. *The Quarrel of Reason with Itself: Essays on Hamann, Michaelis, Lessing, Nietzsche*. Columbia: Camden House, 1988.

Pelters, Wilm. *Lessings Standort: Sinndeutung der Geschichte als Kern seines Denkens*. Heidelberg: Lothar Stiehm Verlag, 1972.

Peters, Brigitte. "Der 17. Literaturbrief und seine Folgen." *Zeitschrift für Germanistik* 10.1 (Februar 1989): 70–75.

Plavius, Heinz. "Revision des Humanismus: Die Wandlungen im Lessing-Bild der Westdeutschen Reaktion." *Neue Deutsche Literatur* 12.9 (1964): 94–109.

Pons, Georges. "Lessing: un érudit malgré lui?" *Recherches Germaniques* 9 (1979): 30–54.

Raabe, Paul. "Die Weimarer Lessing-Bibliographie." *Wolfenbütteler Studien zur Aufklärung* 2 (1975): 331–38.

Rilla, Paul. *Lessing und sein Zeitalter*. München: Verlag C. H. Beck, 1977.

Ritchie, Gisela F. *Der Dichter und die Frau*. Bonn: Bouvier Verlag, 1989.

Ritzel, Wolfgang. *Gotthold Ephraim Lessing*. Stuttgart: W. Kohlhammer Verlag, 1966.

Rüskamp, Wulf. *Dramaturgie ohne Publikum*. Köln: Böhlau Verlag, 1984.

Schenkel, Martin. *Lessings Poetik des Mitleids*. Bonn: Bouvier Verlag Herbert Grundmann, 1984.

Schilson, Arno. "Lessing und die Aufklärung: Notizen zur Forschung." *Theologie und Philosophie* 54 (1979): 379–405.

———. *Lessings Christentum*. Göttingen: Vandenhoeck und Ruprecht, 1980.

Schlegel, Friedrich. *Kritische Friedrich-Schlegel-Ausgabe*. Hsg. Ernst Behler. 35 Bände. Paderborn: Verlag Ferdinand Schöningh, 1967.

Schmidt, Erich. *Lessing: Geschichte seines Lebens und seiner Schriften*. 1. Aufl. 2 Bände. Berlin, 1884–92.

———. *Lessing: Geschichte seines Lebens und seiner Schriften*. 3. Aufl. 2 Bände. Berlin: Weidmannsche Buchhandlung, 1909.

Schmitt-Sasse, Joachim. *Das Opfer der Tugend*. Bonn: Bouvier Verlag Herbert Grundmann, 1983.

Schneider, Heinrich. *Das Buch Lessing*. München: Wilhelm Langewiesche-Brandt, 1929.

———. *Lessing: Zwölf biographische Studien*. Bern: A. Francke Verlag, 1951.

Schöne, Albrecht. "In Sachen des Ungenannten: Lessing contra Goeze." *Text + Kritik: Zeitschrift für Literatur* 26/27 (1970): 1–25.

Schrimpf, Hans Joachim. *Der Schriftsteller als öffentliche Person: Von Lessing bis Hochhuth*. Berlin: Erich Schmidt Verlag, 1977.

Schröder, Jürgen. *Gotthold Ephraim Lessing: Sprache und Drama*. München: Wilhelm Fink Verlag, 1972.

Schulz, Bernhard. "Die Sprache als Kampfmittel: Zur Sprachform von Kampfschriften Luthers, Lessings und Nietzsches." *Deutsche Vierteljahrsschrift für Literaturwissenschaft und Geistesgeschichte* 18 (1940): 431–66.

Schulz, Günter, Hsg. *Lessing und der Kreis seiner Freunde*. Heidelberg: Verlag Lambert Schneider, 1985.

Seeba, Hinrich C. *Die Liebe zur Sache: Öffentliches und privates Interesse in Lessings Dramen*. Tübingen: Max Niemeyer Verlag, 1973.

Seidel, Siegfried. *Gotthold Ephraim Lessing 1729–1781*. Berlin: Verlag Neues Leben, 1963.

Seifert, Siegfried. *Lessing-Bibliographie*. Berlin: Aufbau Verlag, 1973.

Seiffert, H. W. "Neues über Lessings Literaturbriefe." *Festschrift zur 250. Wiederkehr der Geburtstage von Johann Wilhelm Ludwig Gleim und Magnus Gottfried Lichtwer: Beiträge zur deutschen Literatur des 18. Jahrhunderts*. Halberstadt: Gleimhaus, 1969.

Sichelschmidt, Gustav. *Lessing: Der Mann und sein Werk*. Düsseldorf: Droste Verlag, 1989.

Siebert, Donald T. Jr. "Laokoon and Polymetis: Lessing's Treatment of Joseph Spence." *Lessing Yearbook 3*. München: Max Hueber Verlag, 1971.

Simon, Ralf. "Nathans Argumentationsverfahren: Konsequenzen der Fiktionalisierung von Theorie in Lessings Drama *Nathan der Weise*." *Deutsche Vierteljahrsschrift für Literaturwissenschaft und Geistesgeschichte* 65.4 (Dezember 1991): 609–35.

Simpson, Patricia Anne. "Telling Secrets, Telling Truths: Lessing's Theory of Language in *Ernst und Falk. Gespräche für Freimäurer*." *The Journal of the Midwest Modern Language Association* 23.2 (Fall 1990): 17–25.

Stahr, Adolf. *G. E. Lessing: Sein Leben und seine Werke*. 2 Teile. Berlin, 1877.

Staiger, Emil. "Lessings Prosa: Eine Vorlesung." *Dichtung und Deutung: Gedächtnisschrift für Hans M. Wolff*. Hsg. Karl S. Guthke. Bern: A. Francke Verlag, 1961.

Steinmetz, Horst. "Aufklärung und Tragödie: Lessings Tragödien vor dem Hintergrund des Trauerspielmodells der Aufklärung." *Amsterdamer Beiträge zur neueren Germanistik* 1 (1972): 3–41.

———. "Der Kritiker Lessing: Zu Form und Methode der *Hamburgischen Dramaturgie*." *Neophilologus* 52 (1968): 30–48.

———, Hsg. *Lessing—ein unpoetischer Dichter*. Frankfurt: Athenäum Verlag, 1969.

———. "Verstehen, Mißverstehen, Nichtverstehen." *Germanisch-Romanische Monatsschrift* 37.4 (1987): 387–98.

Stephan, Inge. "Frauenbild und Tugendbegriff im bürgerlichen Trauerspiel bei Lessing und Schiller." *Lessing Yearbook 17*. Detroit: Wayne State University Press, 1986.

Stickler, John. "Lessing and the Aura of Censorship: Implications for *Emilia Galotti.*" *Lessing Yearbook 19*. Detroit: Wayne State University Press, 1988.

Strohschneider-Kohrs, Ingrid. *Vom Prinzip des Maßes in Lessings Kritik.* Stuttgart: J. B. Metzlersche Verlagsbuchhandlung, 1969.

Sturges, Beate. *Lessing als Wegbereiter der Emanzipation der Frau.* New York: Peter Lang, 1989.

Ter-Nedden, Gisbert. *Lessings Trauerspiele.* Stuttgart: J. B. Metzlersche Verlagsbuchhandlung, 1986.

Thielicke, Helmut. *Glauben und Denken in der Neuzeit.* Tübingen: J. C. B. Mohr (Paul Siebeck), 1983.

————. "Lessing und Goeze." *Text + Kritik* 26/27 (1970): 39–52.

Tindemans, C. "Neue Wegen in das Lessing-Studium." *Revue Belge de Philologie et d'Histoire/Belgische Tijdschrift voor Filologie en Geschiedenis* 53 (1975): 815–17.

Todorov, Tzvetan. "Poetic Truth: Three Interpretations." *Essays in Criticism: A Quarterly Journal of Literary Criticism* 38.2 (April 1988): 95–113.

Träger, Claus. "Kritizismus und Historizität in Lessings Methode." *Zeitschrift für Germanistik* 1 (1980): 82–94.

Turajew, Sergej. "Lessings Leistung in der europäischen Aufklärung." *Weimarer Beiträge: Zeitschrift für Literaturwissenschaft, Ästhetik und Kulturtheorie* 25.xi (1979): 165–71.

Turk, Horst. *Dialektischer Dialog.* Göttingen: Vandenhoeck und Ruprecht, 1975.

Ugrinsky, Alexej, ed. *Lessing and the Enlightenment.* Westport, Connecticut: Greenwood Press, 1986.

Wagner, Albert Malte. "A Century of Research on Lessing: Past and Future of Modern Languages." *Modern Languages* 25.1 (1943/44): 5–19.

Wehrli, Beatrice. *Kommunikative Wahrheitsfindung: Zur Funktion der Sprache in Lessings Drama.* Tübingen: Max Niemeyer Verlag, 1983.

Wessell, Leonard P., Jr. "*Geist* and *Buchstabe* as Creative Principles in Lessing's Dramaturgy." *Lessing Yearbook 5*. München: Max Hueber Verlag, 1973.

————. *G. E. Lessing's Theology: A Reinterpretation. A Study in the Problematic Nature of the Enlightenment.* The Hague: Mouton and Co., 1977.

von Wiese, Benno, Hsg. *Deutsche Dichter des 18. Jahrhunderts: Ihr Leben und Werk.* Berlin: Erich Schmidt Verlag, 1977.

————. *Lessing: Dichtung, Ästhetik, Philosophie.* Leipzig: Verlag Quelle und Mayer, 1931.

de Wild, Henk. *Tradition und Neubeginn: Lessings Orientierung an der europäischen Tradition.* Amsterdam: Rodopi, 1986.

Wilson, W. Daniel. "'Die Dienste der Grossen': The Flight from Public Service in Lessing's Major Plays." *Deutsche Vierteljahrsschrift für Literaturwissenschaft und Geistesgeschichte* 61.2 (June 1987): 238–65.

Wölfel, K. *Lessings Leben und Werk in Daten und Bildern.* Frankfurt: Insel Verlag, 1967.

Wurst, Karin A. "Abwesenheit-Schweigen-Tötung: Die Möglichkeiten der Frau? Lessings Funktionalisierung literarischer Klischees." *Orbis Litterarum* 45 (1990): 113–27.

————. *Familiale Liebe ist die "wahre Gewalt": Die Repräsentation der Familie in G. E. Lessings dramatischem Werk.* Amsterdam: Rodopi, 1988.

KIERKEGAARD

Agacinski, Sylviane. *Aparte: Conceptions and Deaths of Søren Kierkegaard*. Translated
by Kevin Newmark. Tallahassee: Florida State University Press, 1988.

Ainley, Alison. "The Subject of Ethics: Kierkegaard and Feminist Perspectives on an
'Ethical' Self." *The Oxford Literary Review* 11.1–2 (1989): 169–88.

Alker, Ernst. "Neue Bücher über Sören Kierkegaard." *Literarische Handweiser* 6
(1929/30): 415–24.

Andersen, Vilh. *Tider og Typer af Dansk Aands Historie*. Kjøbenhavn [Copenhagen]:
Gyldendalske Boghandel Nordisk Forlag, 1916.

Anz, Heinrich, Peter Kemp, und Friedrich Schmöe, Hsg. *Kierkegaard und die deutsche
Philosophie seiner Zeit*. München: Wilhelm Fink Verlag, 1980.

Anz, Wilhelm. *Kierkegaard und der deutsche Idealismus*. Tübingen: J. C. B. Mohr, 1956.

Ashbaugh, Anne Freire. "The Singular Individual: Stand-Point of a Renounced Authorship." *Man and World* 19 (1986): 123–41.

Bertelsen, Jes. *Kategori og afgørelse: Strukturer i Kierkegaards taenkning*. Viborg:
Nørhaven Bogtrykkeri a-s, [1972].

Bigelow, Pat. *Kierkegaard and the Problem of Writing*. Tallahassee: The Florida State
University Press, 1987.

Billeskov-Jansen, F. J. "Le Climat Philosophique du Danemark au Temps du Kierkegaard." *Danish Yearbook of Philosophy* 8 (1971): 16–36.

———. "L'Héritage de Kierkegaard dans les pays Nordiques." *Cahiers du Sud* 371 (50
année, Avril-Mai 1963): 18–27.

Blanshard, Brand. "Kierkegaard on Faith." *The Personalist* 49 (Winter 1968): 5–23.

Bloom, Harold, ed. *Søren Kierkegaard*. New York and Philadelphia: Chelsea House
Publishers, 1989.

Bohlin, Torsten. *Sören Kierkegaard: L'Homme et l'Oeuvre*. Trad. P-H. Tisseau. Bazoges-
en-Pareds: Chez le Traducteur, 1941.

Brandes, Georg. *Sören Kierkegaard: Ein literarisches Charakterbild*. 1879. Reprint.
Hildesheim: Georg Olms Verlag, 1975.

Brecht, F. J. "Die Kierkegaardforschung im letzten Jahrfünft." *Literarische Berichte
aus dem Gebiete der Philosophie*. Hsg. Arthur Hoffmann-Erfurt. Erfurt: Verlag
Kurt Stenger, 1931.

Bridg   Thomas. "Derrida, Kierkegaard, and the Orders of Speech." *Philosophy Today*
32 (Summer 1988): 95–109.

Brix, Hans. "Mystica om Søren Kierkegaard." *Analyser og Problemer 3*. København
[Copenhagen]: Gyldendalske Boghandel Nordisk Forlag, 1936.

Brod, Max. *Diesseits und Jenseits*. 2 Bände. Winterthur: Mondial-Verlag Ag., 1947.

Brun, Jean. "Kierkegaard Penseur Tragique." *Les Études Philosophiques* 3 (1963):
299–314.

Buber, Martin. *Die Frage an den Einzelnen*. Berlin: Im Schocken Verlag, 1936.

Campbell, Charles Ray. "The Attack from behind: Irony and Soeren Kierkegaard's Dialectic of Communication." Ph. D dissertation Syracuse University, 1973.

Cappelørn, Niels Jørgen. "Kierkegaards eigener 'Gesichtspunkt' 'Vorwärts zu leben,
aber rückwärts zu verstehen'." *Neue Zeitschrift für systematische Theologie und
Religionsphilosophie* 17 (1975): 61–75.

Chestov, Léon. *Kierkegaard et la philosophie existentielle.* Trad. T. Rageot et B. de Schloezer. Paris: Librairie Philosophique J. Vrin, 1948.

Christopherson, Myrvin Frederick. "Søren Kierkegaard's Dialectic of Communication: An Approach to the Communication of Existential Knowledge." Ph. D. dissertation Purdue University, 1965.

Clair, André. *Pseudonymie et Paradoxe: La pensée dialectique de Kierkegaard.* Paris: Librairie Philosophique J. Vrin, 1976.

Colette, Jacques. "Chronique Kierkegaardienne." *La Revue Nouvelle (Bruxelles)* (15 février 1963): 181–88.

———. "Comptes Rendus. Études Kierkegaardiennes récentes." *Revue Philosophique de Louvain* (février 1972): 116–30.

———. "Expérience, Subjectivité et Langage." *Revue des Sciences Philosophiques et Théologiques* 60 (1976): 625–37.

Collins, James. *The Mind of Kierkegaard.* Chicago: Henry Regnery Company, 1967.

Congar, M. J. "L'actualité de Kierkegaard." *La Vie Intellectuelle* 6 (1934): 9–36.

Connell, George. *To Be One Thing: Personal Unity in Kierkegaard's Thought.* Macon, Ga.: Mercer University Press, 1985.

Creegan, Charles L. *Wittgenstein and Kierkegaard: Religion, Individuality, and Philosophical Method.* London and New York: Routledge, 1989.

Crites, Stephen. *In the Twilight of Christendom.* Chambersburg, Pa.: The American Academy of Religion, 1972.

Croxall, T. H. *Kierkegaard Commentary.* New York: Harper and Brothers, 1956.

Delfgaauw, Bernard. "Literatuuroverzicht de Kierkegaardstudie in Skandinavie." *Tidschrift voor Filosofi* 38 (maart 1976): 136–58.

Dempf, Alois. *Kierkegaards Folgen.* Leipzig: Jakob Hegner, 1935.

Diem, Hermann. *Kierkegaard: An Introduction.* Translated by David Green. Richmond, Va.: John Knox Press, 1966.

———. "Kierkegaard und sein Jahrhundert." *Zeitwende: Die neue Furche* 26 (1955): 727–36.

Dokter, Taeke. *De Structuur van Kierkegaards Oeuvre.* Assen: Van Gorcum en Comp. N.V., 1936.

Dunning, Stephen N. *Kierkegaard's Dialectic of Inwardness: A Structural Analysis of the Theory of Stages.* Princeton: Princeton University Press, 1985.

———. "Rhetoric and Reality in Kierkegaard's *Postscript.*" *International Journal for Philosophy of Religion* 15.3 (1984): 125–37.

Elrod, John W. *Being and Existence in Kierkegaard's Pseudonymous Works.* Princeton: Princeton University Press, 1975.

———. "Climacus, Anti-Climacus, and the Problem of Suffering." *Thought: A Review of Culture and Idea* 55.218 (September 1980): 306–19.

———. *Kierkegaard and Christendom.* Princeton: Princeton University Press, 1981.

Evans, C. Stephen. "Kierkegaard on Subjective Truth: Is God an Ethical Fiction?" *International Journal for Philosophy of Religion* 7.1 (1976): 288–99.

———. *Kierkegaard's "Fragments" and "Postscript": The Religious Philosophy Of Johannes Climacus.* Atlantic Highlands, N.J.: Humanities Press, 1983.

———. "The Relevance of Historical Evidence for Christian Faith: A Critique of a Kierkegaardian View." *Faith and Philosophy* 7.4 (October 1990): 470–85.

Fabro, Cornelio. "La Critica de Kierkegaard al Ochocientos." Translated by Alma Novella Marani. *Sapientia (La Plata)* 5 (1950): 9–18.

Fahrenbach, Helmut. *Die Gegenwärtige Kierkegaard-Auslegung in der deutschsprachigen Literatur von 1948 bis 1962*. Tübingen: J. C. B. Mohr, 1962.

Fausset, Hugh I'Anson. *Poets and Pundits*. New Haven: Yale University Press, 1947.

Ferreira, M. Jamie. "Kierkegaardian Transitions: Paradox and Pathos." *International Philosophical Quarterly* 31.1 (March 91): 65–80.

Fenger, Henning. *Kierkegaard, the Myths and their Origins*. Translated by George C. Schoolfield. New Haven: Yale University Press, 1980.

Fletcher, David Bruce. *Social and Political Perspectives in the Thought of Soren Kierkegaard*. Washington, D.C.: University Press of America, 1982.

Fox, Michael. "Will the Real S. Kierkegaard Please Step Forward?" *Queen's Quarterly* 83.2 (Summer 1976): 367–74.

Friedman, R. Z. "Looking for Abraham: Kierkegaard and the Knight of Anxiety." *International Philosophical Quarterly* 27.3 (September 1987): 249–62.

Galati, Michael. "A Rhetoric for the Subjectivist in a World of Untruth: the Tasks and Strategy of Soren Kierkegaard." *The Quarterly Journal of Speech* 55 (1969): 372–80.

Gardiner, Patrick. *Kierkegaard*. Oxford and New York: Oxford University Press, 1988.

Geismar, D. Eduard. *Sören Kierkegaard*. Göttingen: Vandenhoeck und Ruprecht, 1929.

Gellman, Jerome I. "Kierkegaard's *Fear and Trembling*." *Man and World* 23.3 (July 90): 295–304.

Goicoechea, David. "Kierkegaard on the Existential Person." *Proceedings of the American Catholic Philosophical Association* 60 (1986): 227–32.

Goold, Patrick. "Reading Kierkegaard: Two Pitfalls and a Strategy for avoiding them." *Faith and Philosophy* 7.3 (July 1990): 304–15.

Green, Ronald M. "Abraham, Isaac, and the Jewish Tradition: An Ethical Reappraisal." *The Journal of Religious Ethics* 10.1 (Spring 1982): 1–21.

———. "Deciphering *Fear and Trembling*'s Secret Message." *Religious Studies* 22.1 (March 1986): 95–111.

Grimault, Marguerite. *Kierkegaard par lui-même*. Paris: Éditions du seuil, 1962.

Grimsley, Ronald. *Kierkegaard*. New York: Charles Scribner's Sons, 1973.

Groethuysen, B. "Mythes et Portraits." *Les Essais* 23 (1947): 191–202.

Gusdorf, Georges. *Kierkegaard*. Paris: Éditions Seghers, 1963.

Haecker, Theodor. *Kierkegaard the Cripple*. Translated by C. Van O. Bruyn. New York: Philosophical Library, 1950.

Hannay, Alastair. "A Kind of Philosopher: Comments in Connection with Some Recent Books on Kierkegaard." *Inquiry* 18 (Autumn 1975): 354–65.

———. *Kierkegaard*. London: Routledge and Kegan Paul, 1982.

Hansen, Holger. "Omkring Søren Kierkegaard: Synspunkter og Problemer." *Ord och Bild* 62 (1953): 547–58.

———. "Oversigt over den nyere Kierkegaard-Forskning." *Edda* (1936): 340–51.

Hartshorne, M. Holmes. *Kierkegaard Godly Deceiver: The Nature and Meaning of his Pseudonymous Writings*. New York: Columbia University Press, 1990.

Heiss, Robert. *Hegel. Kierkegaard. Marx*. Translated by E. B. Garside. N.p.: Delacorte Press/Seymour Lawrence, 1975.

Helweg, Hjalmar. *Søren Kierkegaard: En psykiatrisk-psykologisk Studie.* København [Copenhagen]: Hagerup, 1933.

Henriksen, Aage. "Methods and Results of Kierkegaard Studies in Scandinavia." *Publications of the Kierkegaard Society 1.* Copenhagen: Ejnar Munksgaard, 1951.

Himmelstrup, Jens og Kjeld Birket-Smith. *Søren Kierkegaard. International bibliografi.* København [Copenhagen]: Nyt Nordisk Forlag Arnold Busck, 1962.

Hirsch, Emanuel. *Kierkegaard-Studien.* 2 Bände. Gütersloh: Verlag C. Bertelsmann, 1933.

————. *Wege zu Kierkegaard.* Berlin: Verlag "Die Spur" Herbert Dorbandt KG, 1968.

Höffding, Harald. *Sören Kierkegaard als Philosoph.* Stuttgart, 1896.

Hoffmann, W. Michael. "Kierkegaard as a Philosophical Poet." *Midwest Journal of Philosophy* 5 (Spring 1977): 21–30.

Hohlenberg, Johannes. *Sören Kierkegaard.* Translated by T. H. Croxall. New York: Pantheon Books Inc., 1954.

Holm, Kjeld, Malthe Jacobsen og Bjarne Troelsen. *Søren Kierkegaard og Romantikerne.* København [Copenhagen]: Berlingske Forlag, 1974.

Jalota, Indu. "Kierkegaard's Notion of Subjectivity and its Bearing on the Problem of Communication." *Indian Philosophical Quarterly* 7 (April 1980): 393–98.

Jaspers, Karl. *Psychologie der Weltanschauungen.* 3. Aufl. Berlin: Verlag von Julius Springer, 1925.

————. *Vernunft und Existenz.* 1935. München: R. Piper, 1960.

Jensenius, Knud. "Myten om Søren Kierkegaards saedelige Fald." *Festskrift til Vilhelm Andersen: udgivet i anledning af hans halvfjerdsaars Fødselsdag 16. Oktober 1934.* København [Copenhagen]: Gyldendalske Boghandel Nordisk Forlag, 1934.

————. *Nogle Kierkegaardstudier.* Kjøbenhavn [Copenhagen]: Nyt Nordisk Forlag-Arnold Busck, 1932.

Johnson, Howard A. and Niels Thulstrup, eds. *A Kierkegaard Critique.* New York: Harper and Brothers, 1962.

Jolivet, Régis. *Introduction to Kierkegaard.* Translated by W. H. Barber. New York: E. P. Dutton and Co., Inc., n.d.

————. *Kierkegaard.* Übers. Olof Gigon. Bern: A. Francke Verlag, 1948.

Jorgensen, Aage. *Søren Kierkegaard-litteratur 1961–1970.* Aarhus: Akademisk Boghandel, 1971.

————. *Søren Kierkegaard-litteratur 1971–1980.* Aarhus: Nørhaven Bogtrykkeri a/s, 1982.

Kabell, Aage. *Kierkegaardstudiet i Norden.* København [Copenhagen]: H. Hagerup, 1948.

Kaufmann, Walter. "Kierkegaard." *The Kenyon Review* 18.2 (Spring 1956): 182–211.

Kellenberger, J. "Kierkegaard, Indirect Communication, and Religious Truth." *International Journal for Philosophy of Religion* 16.2 (1984): 153–60.

Kirmmse, Bruce H. *Kierkegaard in Golden Age Denmark.* Bloomington and Indianapolis: Indiana University Press, 1990.

Kleinman, Jackie. "Kierkegaard: The Mad Bank-Note." *Dialogue (Phi Sigma Tai)* 18.1 (October 1975): 1–13.

Klemke, E. D. *Studies in the Philosophy of Kierkegaard.* The Hague: Martinus Nikhoff, 1976.

Lang, Théodore et Madeleine Lang. *Kierkegaard (1813–1855) Exposition*. Strasbourg: Bibliotheque Nationale et Universitaire, 1963.

Lapointe, François H. *Sören Kierkegaard and his Critics: An International Bibliography of Criticism*. Westport, Conn.: Greenwood Press, 1980.

Lebowitz, Naomi. *Kierkegaard: A Life of Allegory*. Baton Rouge and London: Louisiana State University Press, 1985.

Levi, Albert William. "The Three Masks." *The Kenyon Review* 18.2 (Spring 1956): 169–82.

Levine, Michael P. "Kierkegaard: What does the Subjective Individual Risk?" *International Journal for Philosophy of Religion* 13 (1982): 13–22.

Lowrie, Walter. *A Short Life of Kierkegaard*. Princeton: Princeton University Press, 1942.

———. *Kierkegaard*. 2 vols. New York: Harper and Bros., 1962.

Lübcke, Poul. "Kierkegaard and Indirect Communication." *History of European Ideas* 12.1 (1990): 31–40.

Mackey, Louis. *Kierkegaard: A Kind of Poet*. Philadelphia: University of Pennsylvania Press, 1971.

———. *Points of View: Readings of Kierkegaard*. Tallahassee: Florida State University Press, 1986.

Magnussen, Rikard. *Det saerlige Kors*. København [Copenhagen]: Ejnar Munksgaard, 1942.

———. *Søren Kierkegaard set udefra*. København [Copenhagen]: Ejnar Munksgaard, 1942.

Malantschuk, Gregor. *Kierkegaard's Thought*. Edited and translated by Howard V. Hong and Edna H. Hong. Princeton: Princeton University Press, 1971.

———. *The Controversial Kierkegaard*. Translated by Howard V. Hong and Edna H. Hong. Waterloo, Ontario: Wilfrid Laurier University Press, 1980.

Marquet, Jean-François. "Le Message et son Labyrinthe." *Critique* 222 (novembre 1965), 950–64.

Marsh, James L. "Interiority and Revolution." *Philosophy Today* 29.3/4 (Fall 1985): 191–202.

———. "The two Kierkegaards." *Philosophy Today* 16 (Winter 1972): 313–22.

Martinez, Roy. "Kierkegaard's Ideal of Inward Deepening." *Philosophy Today* 32 (Summer 88): 110–17.

———. "Socrates and Judge Wilhelm: A Case of Kierkegaardian Ethics." *Philosophy Today* 34.1 (Spring 90): 39–47.

McKinnon, Alastair, ed. *Kierkegaard: Resources and Results*. Montreal, Ontario: Wilfrid Laurier University Press, 1982.

———. "Some Minor Figures in Kierkegaard's Works." *International Studies in Philosophy* 11 (1979): 165–73.

McLane, Earl. "Kierkegaard and Subjectivity." *International Journal for Philosophy of Religion* 8.4 (1977): 211–32.

Mesnard, Pierre. *Le Vrai Visage de Kierkegaard*. Paris: Beauchesne et ses Fils, 1948.

Michalson, Gordon E., Jr. "Theology, Historical Knowledge, and the Contingency-Necessity Distinction." *International Journal for Philosophy of Religion* 14.2 (1983): 87–98.

Mooney, Edward F. "Kierkegaard, Our Contemporary: Reason, Subjectivity, and the Self." *The Southern Journal of Philosophy* 27.3 (Fall 1989): 381–97.

———. *Knights of Faith and Resignation: Reading Kierkegaard's "Fear and Trembling."* Albany: State University of New York Press, 1991.

Moore, W. G. "Recent Studies of Kierkegaard." *The Journal of Theological Studies* 40 (July 1939): 225–31.

Morris, T. F. "Kierkegaard's Understanding of Socrates." *International Journal for Philosophy of Religion* 19.1–2 (1986): 105–11.

Nielsen, Edith Ortmann og Niels Thulstrup. *Søren Kierkegaard: Bidrag til en Bibliografi.* København [Copenhagen]: Ejnar Munksgaard, 1951.

Nordentoft, Kresten. *"Hvad siger Brand-Majoren?": Kierkegaards opgør med sin samtid.* København: G. D. C. GAD, 1973.

Ostenfeld, Ib. *Søren Kierkegaard's Psychology.* Translated by Alastair McKinnon. 1972. Reprint. Waterloo, Ontario: Wilfrid Laurier University Press, 1978.

Outka, Gene. "Equality and Individuality: Thoughts on two Themes in Kierkegaard." *The Journal of Religious Ethics* 10.2 (Fall 1982): 171–203.

Pattison, George. "A Drama of Love and Death: Michael Pedersen Kierkegaard and Regine Olsen Revisited." *History of European Ideas* 12.1 (1990): 79–91.

Perkins, Robert L. "Always Himself: A Survey of Recent Kierkegaard Literature." *Southern Journal of Philosophy* 12.4 (Winter 1974): 539–51.

———, ed. *International Kierkegaard Commentary: The Sickness Unto Death.* Macon, Ga.: Mercer University Press, 1987.

———. "Kierkegaard, a Kind of Epistemologist." *History of European Ideas* 12.1 (1990): 7–18.

———, ed. *Kierkegaard's "Fear and Trembling": Critical Appraisals.* University: The University of Alabama Press, 1981.

Petersen, Erik Schmidt. *Søren Kierkegaard i Nutiden og i samtiden.* Faaborg: Nertman og Brandts Forlag, 1950.

Plekon, Michael. "'Anthropological Contemplation': Kierkegaard and Modern Social Theory." *Thought: A Review of Culture and Idea* 55.218 (September 1980): 346–69.

———. "Beyond Existentialist Caricatures: New Views Of Kierkegaard." *Human Studies* 4 (January–March 1981): 87–95.

———. "'Other Kierkegaards'—New Views and Reinterpretations in Scholarship." *Thought: A Review of Culture and Idea* 55.218 (September 1980): 370–75.

Pojman, Louis P. "Kierkegaard on Faith and History." *International Journal for Philosophy of Religion* 13.2 (1982): 57–68.

———. "Kierkegaard on Subjectivity: Two Concepts." *Philosophical Topics*, no vol. (Supp. 80): 39–52.

———. *The Logic of Subjectivity: Kierkegaard's Philosophy of Religion.* University: The University of Alabama Press, 1984.

Price, George. *The Narrow Pass.* New York: McGraw-Hill Book Company, Inc., 1963.

Przywara, Erich. *Das Geheimnis Kierkegaards.* München: R. Oldenbourg, 1929.

Quinn, Philip L. "Agamemnon and Abraham: The Tragic Dilemma of Kierkegaard's Knight of Faith." *Literature & Theology: An Interdisciplinary Journal of Theory and Criticism.* 4.2 (July 1990): 181–93.

Richter, Liselotte. *Der Begriff der Subjektivität bei Kierkegaard*. Würzburg: Verlag Konrad Triltsch, 1934.

———. "Konstruktives und Destruktives in der neuesten Kierkegaard-Forschung." *Theologische Literaturzeitung* 77 (1952): 141–48.

Roberts, Robert C. *Faith, Reason, and History: Rethinking Kierkegaard's "Philosophical Fragments"*. Macon, Ga.: Mercer University Press, 1986.

———. "Thinking Subjectively." *International Journal for the Philosophy of Religion* 11. (Summer 1980): 71–92.

Rohatyn, Dennis A. "Kierkegaard and his Critics." *Two Dogmas of Philosophy and other Essays in the Philosophy of Philosophy*. Rutherford, N.J.: Fairleigh Dickinsen University Press, 1977.

Rohde, H. P. *Gaadefulde Stadier paa Kierkegaards Wej*. København [Copenhagen]: Rosenkilde og Bagger, 1974.

Rohde, Peter P. *Sören Kierkegaard in Selbstzeugnissen und Bilddokumenten*. Übers. Thyra Dohrenburg. Hamburg: Rowohlt Taschenbuch Verlag, 1959.

Rosenow, Eliyahu. "Kierkegaard's Existing Individual." *Journal of Philosophy of Education* 23.1 (1989): 3–13.

———. "Kierkegaard's Mirror." *Educational Philosophy and Theory* 22.1 (1990): 8–15.

Rubow, Paul V. *Kierkegaard og hans Samtidige*. København [Copenhagen]: Gyldendalske Boghandel Nordisk Forlag, 1950.

Ruttenbeck, Walter. *Sören Kierkegaard: Der christliche Denker und sein Werk*. Berlin: Trowitzsch und Sohn, 1929.

Sales, Michel. "Dix Ans de Publications Kierkegaardiennes en Langue Française." *Archives de Philosophie* 35 (octobre–décembre 1972): 649–72.

Sandok, Theresa A. "Kierkegaard on Irony and Humor." Ph. D. dissertation Notre Dame, 1975.

Sarf, Harold. "Reflections on Kierkegaard's Socrates." *Journal of the History of Ideas* 44.2 (April–June 1983): 255–76.

Schacht, Richard. "Kierkegaard on 'Truth is Subjectivity' and 'The Leap of Faith.' *Canadian Journal of Philosophy* 2.3 (March 1973): 297–313.

Schalow, Frank. "Temporality Revisited: Kierkegaard and the Transitive Character of Time." *Auslegung* 17.1 (Winter 91): 15–25.

Scheier, Claus-Artur. "Klassische und existentielle Ironie: Platon und Kierkegaard." *Philosophisches Jahrbuch der Görres-Gesellschaft* (Freiburg FRG) 97.2 (1990): 238–50.

Schleifer, Ronald and Robert Markley, eds. *Kierkegaard and Literature: Irony, Repetition, and Criticism*. Norman: University of Oklahoma Press, 1984.

Shmuëli, Adi. *Kierkegaard and Consciousness*. Translated by Naomi Handelman. Princeton: Princeton University Press, 1971.

Silverman, Hugh J., ed. *Writing the Politics of Difference*. Albany: State University of New York Press, 1991.

Sløk, Johannes. "Afmytologisering af Kierkegaard." *Dansk Teologisk Tidsskrift* 40 (1977): 120–27.

Smith, Joseph H., ed. *Kierkegaard's Truth: The Disclosure of the Self*. New Haven and London: Yale University Press, 1981.

Sontag, Frederick. *A Kierkegaard Handbook*. Atlanta: John Knox Press, 1979.

————. "Strange Interlude." *Man and World* 21.2 (March 1988): 213–21.

Søren Kierkegaard i hundredaaret for hans død: Mindeudstilling. København [Copenhagen]: Kongelige Bibliothek, 1955.

Stack, George J. "The Meaning of 'Subjectivity is Truth'." *Midwest Journal of Philosophy* (Spring 1975): 26–40.

Starobinski, Jean. "Kierkegaard et les Masques." *La Nouvelle Revue Française* (I) 13e année 148 (1er Avril 1965): 607–22 (II) 13e année 149 (1er Mai 1965): 809–25.

Stybe, Svend Erik. "Trends in Danish Philosophy." *Journal of the British Society for Phenomenology* 4.2 (May 1973): 153–70.

Swenson, David F. *Something about Kierkegaard*. Minneapolis: Augsburg Publishing House, 1941 and 1945.

Taylor, Mark C. *Journeys to Selfhood: Hegel and Kierkegaard*. Berkeley: University of California Press, 1980.

————. *Kierkegaard's Pseudonymous Authorship: A Study of Time and the Self*. Princeton: Princeton University Press, 1975.

Thibon, Gustave. "Le Drame de Kierkegaard." *Études Carmelitaines* 1 (1938): 140–50.

Thomas, J. Heywood. *Subjectivity and Paradox*. Oxford: Basil Blackwell, 1957.

Thompson, Josiah. *Kierkegaard*. London: Victor Gollancz Ltd., 1974.

————, ed. *Kierkegaard: A collection of Critical Essays*. Garden City, N.Y.: Anchor Books–Doubleday and Co., Inc., 1972.

————. *The Lonely Labyrinth: Kierkegaard's Pseudonymous Works*. Carbondale and Edwardsville: Southern Illinois University Press, 1967.

Thulstrup, Marie Mikulová. *Concepts and Alternatives in Kierkegaard*. "Bibliotheca Kierkegaardiana" Vol. 3. Copenhagen: C. A. Reitzels Boghandel, 1980.

Thulstrup, Niels and Marie Mikulová Thulstrup, eds. *Kierkegaard and Human Values*. "Bibliotheca Kierkegaardiana" Vol. 7. Copenhagen: C. A. Reitzels Boghandel, 1980.

———— and Marie Mikulová Thulstrup, eds. *Kierkegaard and Speculative Idealism*. "Bibliotheca Kierkegaardiana" Vol. 4. Copenhagen: C. A. Reitzels Boghandel, 1979.

————. *Kierkegaard's Relation to Hegel*. Translated by George L. Stengren. Princeton: Princeton University Press, 1980.

———— and Marie Mikulová Thulstrup, eds. *The Legacy and Interpretation of Kierkegaard*. "Bibliotheca Kierkegaardiana" Vol. 8. Copenhagen: C. A. Reitzels Boghandel, 1981.

Thust, Martin. "Das Marionettentheater Sören Kierkegaards." *Zeitwende* 1 (1925): 18–38.

————. *Sören Kierkegaard: Der Dichter des Religiösen*. München: C. H. Beck'sche Verlagsbuchhandlung, 1931.

Updike, John. "The Fork." *The New Yorker*. 26. February 1966.

Wahl, Jean. *Études Kierkegaardiennes*. 3ème éd. Paris: Librairie Philosophique J. Vrin, 1967.

Walker, Jeremy. *Kierkegaard: The Descent into God*. Kingston and Montreal: McGill–Queen's University Press, 1985.

Westphal, Merold. *Kierkegaard's Critique of Reason and Society*. Macon, Ga.: Mercer University Press, 1987.

————. "Kierkegaard's Politics." *Thought: A Review of Culture and Idea* 55.218 (September 1980): 320–32.

Whittaker, John H. "Kierkegaard and Existence Communications." *Faith and Philosophy* 5.2 (April 1988): 168–84.

Wisdo, David. "Kierkegaard on Belief, Faith, and Explanation." *International Journal for Philosophy of Religion* 21.2 (1987): 95–114.

Zelechow, Bernard. "Fear and Trembling and Joyful Wisdom—The Same Book: A Look at Metaphoric Communication." *History of European Ideas* 12.1 (1990): 93–104.

Index